Ecclesiastes

Wisdom for Living Well

AN IN-DEPTH BIBLE STUDY

by **Courtney Joseph**
with Beverly Wise

Ecclesiastes: Wisdom for Living Well

© 2015 Women Living Well Ministries, LLC

Table of Contents

Preface 1

Week 1-Introduction and Overview 3
Day 1—The Author 4
Day 2—Your Story 8
Day 3—A God Encounter 11
Day 4—Solomon's Failures 15
Day 5—Let's Begin 18

Week 2-Ecclesiastes 1 & 2 22
Day One—Examining the Earth 23
Day Two—The Vanity of Wisdom 28
Day Three—The Vanity of Pleasure 33
Day Four—Comparing Wisdom and Folly 38
Day Five—The Vanity of Work 42

Week 3-Ecclesiastes 3 & 4 45
Day One—A Time for Everything 46
Day Two—He Makes All Things Beautiful 50
Day Three—Injustice and Death 54
Day Four—Affliction and Competition 58
Day Five—Friendships and a Fickle Crowd 62

Week 4-Ecclesiastes 5, 6 & 7 66

Day One—Dreaming To the Glory of God 67

Day Two—Enjoying the Simple Things 71

Day Three—Craving More 75

Day Four—Ending Well 79

Day Five—Choosing What Is Best 84

Week 5-Ecclesiastes 8, 9 & 10:1-10 87

Day 1—It's Time to Shine 88

Day 2—Our God is Good 92

Day 3—Finding Joy 96

Day 4—The Wisest of All 100

Day 5—Avoid Folly 104

Week 6-Ecclesiastes 10:10-20, 11 & 12 107

Day 1—Working Smarter Not Harder 108

Day 2—Living By Faith 113

Day 3—It's Good to Be Alive 117

Day 4—Remember God In Your Youth 121

Day 5—Fear God and Keep His Commandments 125

Video One —Notes 129

Video Two—Notes 130

Video Three—Notes 131

Video Four—Notes 132

Video Five—Notes 133

Video Six—Notes 134

Preface

It was my first day in Greek Class at the Moody Bible Institute. The professor slowly went around the room giving each of us a Greek nickname for the school year. He looked at me and asked, "what is your name?"

"Courtney Wise", I answered.

"Are you wise, Miss Courtney?"

I thought silently to myself, like I've never heard that one before...

"I try to be."

"Then Miss Sophos will be your name in this class."

Miss Sophos.

I liked it.

In the Greek language, the word "Sophos" means wise. For the first 21 years of my life, I walked around with the name 'Miss Wise' but this was ironic because I never felt very wise.

I had always been a bubbly, person who didn't always mind her p's and q's when chatting with her friends. So I'm pretty sure, "wise" would not be a word used to describe me except that everywhere I went, I was known as Courtney Wise.

In contrast, there was my mother, Beverly Wise. Her last name has always seemed more appropriate than mine. My Mom always had her Bible on the kitchen table with colored pencils and notebooks filled to the brim with her reflections from God's word. As a child, I was amazed how verses seemed to roll off her tongue at the most appropriate times.

Since I was a little girl, I've been a witness to her walk with the Lord. She is steadfast and firm in her faith. She is forever a student of the word and seeking to know more about her first love. She is a wise teacher not only to her three daughters but to hundreds of women who have attended her Bible Studies over the last 35 years.

It is my honor to write this Bible study with my mother, my first teacher of God's word. As a little girl at the age of 5, I folded my hands and prayed with her to become a believer.

I have been on a long journey and pursuit for wisdom. I devour God's word in the morning, read Christian books regularly, scour the Internet for devotionals and meaty sermons to listen to, and seek out older women to teach me the things I don't know.

Look how far God has brought the two of us! Oh—only God could use this babbling girl, who thought she'd never learn how to control her tongue, to write a Bible Study!

My mother took the assignment of doing research for this Bible Study on faith, nine months before I began writing. While I finished up my very first book launch—she was faithfully studying and preparing for you all, to meet us here at this time. Her words are woven into mine.

So here we go.

Let's begin this journey toward becoming women living well, as we grow in wisdom and our walk with the King!

Courtney

Week 1~Introduction and Overview

Verse of the Day:

I came that they may have life

and have it abundantly.

John 10:10

Day 1—The Author

Many of us have lives that are full. We have full bellies, full closets, full calendars, full trashcans, full purses and full email inboxes. But at the end of the day, we are empty. God made us all with a built in desire to find the meaning to life and to spend time on things that are meaningful.

Ecclesiastes 1:8 says:

"All things are full of weariness; a man cannot utter it; the eye is not satisfied with seeing, nor the ear filled with hearing."

Isn't it interesting that daily we can hop on our computers and click and click and click from thing to thing to thing and always find something intriguing to look at. Then we can flip on the television and do the same. The eye is never satisfied with seeing nor is the ear filled with hearing. We could literally spend all our time entertaining ourselves. We are desperate to fill ourselves up.

I love reading the Little House on the Prairie Series to my children at bedtime. We are currently in book #5. We have spent many hours reading about the sweet Ingalls family. Each night as I read, I sense a tug at my heart. Their lives were so simple and yet they were so happy. The Ingalls family found contentment in the midst of hardship and fearful times. They possessed joy, love, and perseverance and each night they inspire me to remember that it is the simple things that can bring us the greatest joys in life.

While I love all the amazing analogies I could use from Little House on the Prairie as parallels to our lives, I must be honest. This study we are about to embark on, is not so sweet. The straight talk from Ecclesiastes will rock you to the core. We are going to be real here. It is when we are most open with our inner struggles that genuine life change takes place.

And so I am very excited for this 6-week journey we will take together through the book of Ecclesiastes.

So let's begin:

The word "Ecclesiastes" in the Hebrew is *Qoheleth* (ko-hel-eth) which means: the preacher, the teacher or an official speaker who calls together an assembly.

The Greek word for "assembly" is "*ekklesia*", the New Testament word for church.

This gives us the English title of the book, Ecclesiastes!

ABOUT THE AUTHOR:

It's important when we study any book of the Bible, we first determine the author, the time in history it was written and the purpose.

The traditional view is that King Solomon is the author of Ecclesiastes, although not all scholars agree. Let's observe the details that point to Solomon as author.

Read Ecclesiastes 1:1. The author never calls himself by name. What are the three qualities he used to describe himself?

Look at Ecclesiastes 1:16 and 2:9. What do these verses tell us about the author?

Now look at Ecclesiastes 12:9. What did the Preacher teach the people?

Now let's compare what we learned above about the author to what the Bible says about Solomon in I Kings 4:29-34. How are the two similar?

In Ecclesiastes 2:4-10 the author describes his vast wealth. Describe his life below:

Now compare this to the wealth of Solomon in I Kings 10:21-27

Solomon reigned as Israel's king from approximately 970-930 BC. Most likely Solomon wrote Ecclesiastes near the end of his life as he looked back and reflected on his life.

I am so grateful a man wiser and more wealthy than all of us sought meaning in all the wrong places and wrote all of his experiences in a journal, so thousands of years later we can be saved the heartache of seeking fulfillment in all the wrong places.

DISCUSSION QUESTION:

Is your life full? Do you struggle with feeling too full yet empty? In what ways?

Write a prayer of commitment to God, asking Him to help you complete every page of this study so you can be filled up by His living word and never empty again!

There is only one who can satisfy—the Lord Jesus Christ.

Jesus said to her, *"Everyone who drinks of this water will be thirsty again, but whoever drinks of the water that I will give him will never be thirsty again. The water that I will give him will become in him a spring of water welling up to eternal life."* John 4:13,14

We will only live well, when we drink from the living well, the living words of God. Let's strive to be women living well as we walk with the King!

Verse of the Day:

For everyone who calls

on the name of the Lord

will be saved.

Romans 10:13

Day 2—Your Story

My husband grew up in a home where his parents were divorced. As a result, he spent his teen years living at his grandmother's house. My husband's story begins with his parent's story. Their struggles became his struggles, as he grappled with his little world falling apart.

We all have a story. Our stories always start with our mother and father and our childhood struggles and victories. This is what shapes us. And so today we want to understand what shaped the author of Ecclesiastes.

Read 2 Samuel 11:1-5; 14-17. What did Solomon's parents do wrong?

We see in the passage above, Solomon's father David not only had an affair and had the husband murdered but Bathsheba got pregnant. Oh friends, this was not good. Clearly, this displeased the Lord.

What happened to this baby according to 2 Samuel 12:15-18?

Now read about the birth of Solomon in 2 Samuel 12:24.

The Hebrew name for Solomon is Shalom which means peace. After David repented of his sin (2 Samuel 12:1-14, and Psalm 51), he now had found peace with God.

Peace.

Don't we all long to find peace—peace with God, peace with others and peace from our inner turmoil? As we read Solomon's journals in Ecclesiastes we will see a man in search of peace and in the end, he finds it.

DISCUSSION QUESTION:

Do you have peace today? Why or why not?

All generations of people across time investigate and explore real life issues and questions. Questions like: Who am I? Why am I here? What is the meaning and purpose of my life?

What is your parent's story and how does it intertwine with your story? Did they have peace?

We are not alone in our struggles to find satisfaction. For centuries man has yearned for it.

Jesus said, "I came that they may have life and have it abundantly." (John 10:10b)

Jesus is the only true source of life, and He gives it to the FULL! Have you chosen to follow Jesus? What is the promise of Romans 10:13?

Once you are saved, your story changes! The peace of God is with you. He makes all things new! Apart from faith in the Son of God, Jesus Christ, there is no satisfaction in this life "under the sun".

Hang in there with me through these next 6 weeks as we begin to live the satisfied, abundant, meaningful life that is only found in God.

Verse of the Day:

But seek first the kingdom of God

and his righteousness,

and all these things

will be added to you.

Matthew 6:33

Day 3—A God Encounter

DISCUSSION QUESTION:

Do you remember the day or season of life when you encountered God for the first time? Write about it here.

I was just 5 years old when I confessed my sins and placed my faith in Jesus' sacrifice on the cross and believed in His resurrection.

Maybe you were 6 years old or maybe you were 36 years old. Either way, that was when Jesus became the Lord of your life.

In 1 Kings chapters one and two, we read the story of Solomon being anointed as King and the final words of his father David's advice to him. David told Solomon:

> *"Be strong, and show yourself a man, and keep the charge of the Lord your God, walking in his ways and keeping his statutes, his commandments, his rules, and his testimonies, as it is written in the Law of Moses, that you may prosper in all that you do and wherever you turn." I Kings 2:2-3 (esv)*

Then David died and his son, Solomon, sat on the throne.

A significant spiritual experience occurred in Solomon's life when God appeared to him in a dream. God told Solomon to ask for whatever he wanted, and God would give it to him.

What did Solomon ask for according to I Kings 3:5-15?

Solomon would have been in his late teens or early 20's when he became the King of Israel. He humbly knew he needed wisdom to govern Israel but if God asked you that same question at that young age—would you have answered wisdom?

What do you think you would have asked for?

God was pleased with Solomon's request for wisdom and granted it. God also added additional blessings Solomon did not ask for including great riches and honor. According to 2 Chronicles 1:12, Solomon would become the wisest and wealthiest man who ever lived. He would have no equal.

Do you ever wish God would grant you this same wisdom—and maybe add in some riches and honor as a bonus? Me too!

Turn to the New Testament and read Jesus' words in Matthew 6:28-34. Here Jesus mentions Solomon and his wealth. What does Jesus say 3 times we ought not to be?

My mother is one of the most content people I have ever met. Matthew 6:33 is her life verse and she had my sisters and I memorize this verse when we were very young. It is tucked in my heart forever.

What does Matthew 6:33 say we should seek?

Is there something you are anxious about today?

Write a prayer handing over your worries to God.

I am so proud of you for committing to do this Bible study with us. Let's make it a point to start our days on our knees in prayer seeking God first. Keep digging into God's word and seeking His righteousness first. Watch how God transforms your anxious thoughts into peace. Pursue peace by pursuing Him—the King of Kings.

Verse of the Day:

Unless the Lord builds the house,

those who build it labor in vain.

Psalm 127:1

Day 4—Solomon's Failures

Today is our final day to peek into the "behind the scenes" life of the author Solomon. Tomorrow we will begin our study in Ecclesiastes.

Not only was Solomon the son of a King, a wise and wealthy man, but he also was famous. Let's face it, Solomon had it ALL!

Solomon oversaw many building projects during his reign, the greatest of which was the magnificent First Temple in Jerusalem, the House of the Lord. This was God's dwelling place on earth among His people for 400 years.

During Solomon's reign, Israel experienced a period of peace, prosperity and security. Solomon's fame spread throughout the world, and many came from far and wide to hear his wisdom. (I Kings 4:34)

Solomon is also known for being the author of a major portion of the wisdom literature in the Old Testament. Solomon wrote the book of Proverbs, the Song of Songs, Psalm 72 and 127 and of course Ecclesiastes.

Even though Solomon had all these great successes, he experienced some failure.

Solomon did not obey God's commands given for the king. Can you believe it? After all God had done for him, he sinned in the areas of wealth and women.

Read Deuteronomy 17:16,17. What were 3 of the laws God had for Israel's King?

Solomon violated the Lord's command and owned vast numbers of horses (I Kings 10:25-26,28) and Scripture states that silver was as common as stones in Jerusalem during his reign. (I Kings 10:27)

In the area of women, Solomon had a huge problem. How many wives did he have and what happened as a result according to I Kings 11:3?

I know of so many spiritual leaders who began well…but did not finish well. Somewhere along the way, pride enters in and the leader falls to temptation. In the same way, we see that Solomon's life and reign began well, but did not end well.

I Kings 11:9-14a states:

> *"9 And the Lord was angry with Solomon, because his heart had turned away from the Lord, the God of Israel, who had appeared to him twice 10 and had commanded him concerning this thing, that he should not go after other gods. But he did not keep what the Lord commanded. 11 Therefore the Lord said to Solomon, "Since this has been your practice and you have not kept my covenant and my statutes that I have commanded you, I will surely tear the kingdom from you and will give it to your servant. 12 Yet for the sake of David your father I will not do it in your days, but I will tear it out of the hand of your son. 13 However, I will not tear away all the kingdom, but I will give one tribe to your son, for the sake of David my servant and for the sake of Jerusalem that I have chosen." 14 And the Lord raised up an adversary against Solomon."*

God had personally appeared to Solomon, He had blessed him greatly, yet Solomon failed to obey God's commands. As a result, Israel would be divided after Solomon's death because of his sin against God.

DISCUSSION QUESTIONS:

What do we learn about God's character, His heart, and His ways regarding His relationship with Solomon?

How does this transfer in your own life? What have you learned about the character of God, His heart and His ways regarding your relationship with Him?

This brings us to the end of our background study of the author of Ecclesiastes. At the end of Solomon's life he appears to be reviewing and reflecting upon his successes and failures. During his time on earth "under the sun" he searched for the true meaning of life and he found it!

Isn't it wonderful we don't have to go looking in all the wrong places. Solomon already did that for us! I can't wait to get into Ecclesiastes with you tomorrow!

Verse of the Day:

Do your best to present yourself

to God as one approved

a worker who has no need to be ashamed,

rightly handling the word of truth.

2 Timothy 2:15

Day 5—Let's Begin

Since I was a wee child, the number one tool I watched my mom use during her quiet time were her colored pencils! Mom always had her Bible, Bible study notebook and a set of colored pencils on our kitchen table and if you walked into her kitchen today, you'd probably find them there!

She examines each word and marks key words with different colors or symbols. She numbers lists. She marks sentences where the scripture compares and contrasts different things. She looks up the original definition of the Hebrew and Greek words and writes it in the margins and when something doesn't make sense, she goes to her commentaries, Bible Dictionaries or other versions of the Bible to figure out what God is saying. Mom works hard at understanding scripture and I pray you will put that sort of effort into this study!

Do your best to present yourself to God as one approved, a worker who has no need to be ashamed, rightly handling the word of truth. 2 Timothy 2:15 (esv)

Throughout this study we are going to do some coloring. We will be using the English Standard Version (ESV) since it is a close word for word translation of the original scriptures. This color coding is optional. You can do it in your Bible, purchase a special Bible just for color coding or print out the book of Ecclesiastes from the internet. Do whatever works best for you. The point of color coding is to help us slow down and soak in God's Word, as we read it carefully.

Open your Bible to Ecclesiastes 1 verse 1. Mark it orange.

As we saw on day one, the author introduces himself as the Preacher, son of David and King of Jerusalem.

Now read verse 2, and mark it blue.

In the original language of Hebrew, the word "hebel", is used for vanity, which means emptiness.

In scripture when we see that Jesus is the Lord of Lords or the King of Kings it shows superiority or the greatness of Jesus. In this case—repeating the term "vanity of vanities" shows that life is extremely vain. It can feel extremely empty and futile.

Now read Ecclesiastes 1:3 and mark it blue as well.

GMG BIBLE COLORING CHART

COLORS	KEYWORDS
PURPLE	God, Jesus, Holy Spirit, Saviour, Messiah
PINK	women of the Bible, family, marriage, parenting, friendship, relationships
RED	love, kindness, mercy, compassion, peace, grace
GREEN	faith, obedience, growth, fruit, salvation, fellowship, repentance
YELLOW	worship, prayer, praise, doctrine, angels, miracles, power of God, blessings
BLUE	wisdom, teaching, instruction, commands
ORANGE	prophecy, history, times, places, kings, genealogies, people, numbers, covenants, vows, visions, oaths, future
BROWN/GRAY	Satan, sin, death, hell, evil, idols, false teachers, hypocrisy, temptation

The most important phrase in understanding the text of Ecclesiastes is the term "under the sun", which is used 29 times. This reveals the perspective of the author, as he journals his search for meaning in wealth and wisdom and projects and women and anything...but God.

When we search "under the sun" for meaning—all we find is an empty treadmill with nothing that satisfies. Why? Because we must look ABOVE the sun for our answers.

But isn't that how we live sometimes? We move from thing to thing, searching for the next rainbow, the next high, the next vacation, the next girls night out, the next shopping trip, the next steak dinner, or the next spa day. We chase after the wind rather than chasing our Savior. Nothing "under the sun" can satisfy our souls like knowing and walking with the King.

We know this in our heads but do we live like we believe this?

We live in a culture that doesn't believe people need God except for in a time of crisis. Even then, it's a time to blame God or be angry with Him rather than humble ourselves before Him. But this sort of living only leads to further confusion, depression and disillusionment in this life "under the sun."

Let's look ahead.

I am the type of person who never peeks ahead to see how a story will finish. I like to enjoy the unfolding journey without any spoilers. But today we are going to make an exception.

Open to Ecclesiastes 12:13 &14, to the final words of Solomon.

What 2 things does Solomon conclude in verse 13?

We will look deeper into this passage later, but for now—you know where we are headed. While our journey through Ecclesiastes will cause us to wrestle with the reality of life "under the sun", we are not left without hope. Ecclesiastes 12:13 opens the door to joy and peace and hope like none other.

Let's not wait 6 weeks to find God—let's start with God!

"Jesus said, 'I am the way, and the truth, and the life. No one comes to the Father except through me'. John 14:6 (esv)

The truth of Jesus's death on the cross has made a way for us to live an abundant life free of emptiness! He gives us forgiveness of our sins, a personal relationship with Him, and a hope of eternal life in heaven.

DISCUSSION QUESTION:

Read John 3:16. What does this passage mean to you?

As we strive to be women living well, may we never forget that Jesus is our living well. He is our living water. We must go to Him daily to be refreshed.

Let's close our week in prayer.

Dear Heavenly Father,

You are so good. Thank you for the sacrifice of your Son and the forgiveness of our sins. Forgive us for putting our hope and trust in the wrong things. Help us not to chase after empty and futile things and open our eyes and hearts to understand your word clearly. Change us and make us more like you. May we find joy and peace in your presence and a life full of meaning for your glory.

In the strong name of Jesus we pray, Amen.

Week 2~Ecclesiastes 1 & 2

Verse of the Day:

Therefore, my beloved brothers,

be steadfast, immovable,

always abounding in the work of the Lord,

knowing that in the Lord

your labor is not in vain.

1 Corinthians 15:58

Day One—Examining the Earth
Ecclesiastes 1: 1-11

Let's begin with prayer.

Slowly read or color-code Ecclesiastes 1:1-11.

There is no right or wrong way to do the coloring. It is simply a tool to help us slow down and soak in every Word of God. (Most of mine is blue and orange.)

We all thirst for something new and exciting. The monotony of waking up, packing lunches, perhaps going to work, then making dinner, doing laundry, cleaning up the house, rocking babies and going to bed—just to wake and repeat this cycle again and again, can feel overwhelmingly hard, meaningless and boring. Sometimes it feels like we eat to work and work to eat.

If a woman admitted she was bored with her life, in our culture, her friends would tell her to get busy. Busyness seems to be where we find meaning. So we chase after education, money, fame, relationships, or the next party and end up still on the road to emptiness.

Ecclesiastes 1:3 says: *"What does a man gain by all the toil at which he toils under the sun?"* Then Solomon seeks to answer his own question.

In verse 4, we see Solomon contrasts the earth with the generations of mankind that come and go. While new babies are being born, the old pass away and the cycle continues. Remember, Solomon is writing from an "under the sun" perspective rather an "above the sun" perspective.

Read verses 4-7. What parts of nature display the weariness of life?

For centuries the earth, sun, wind and water have been moving in constant repetition, without getting anywhere.

Do you ever feel like your life is in constant repetition?

The seasons come and go. The sun shines and we go swimming and on vacation, then fall arrives and we pull out the cozy sweaters and mugs of cider, then snow falls and I pull out my crockpot and make some soup, then spring arrives and the tulips bloom once again.

The sun comes up and goes down, year in and year out in constant repetition.

In our boredom we decide to pursue a dream—maybe it's a new car. We get it and 3 years later it's old and we search for a new car. Or maybe it's a degree. We achieve it...then what? We look for the perfect job. Then what? It's not so perfect so we pursue a Master's degree. Then what? We pursue a job. Then what? We get laid off and we pursue another one. Then what? We are always in pursuit...never satisfied.

DISCUSSION QUESTION:

Do you struggle with the monotony of life? Do you feel the urge to always seek out something new?

When Solomon looked "under the sun", he concluded that work was just wearisome and a chasing after the wind. Let's take a look "above the sun" at God's view of work.

Look up these references and write out God's view of work.

Colossians 3:23

I Corinthians 15:58

God ordained work in the Garden of Eden. It is a good thing but after Adam sinned, we read in Genesis 3:17b these words *"cursed is the ground because of you; in pain you shall eat of it all the days of your life."*

Work was always a part of God's plan but because of sin, work brings sweat and sorrow. Should we conclude that all work is vain?

No, it has value for this life and the next. It is work that is done *to the glory of God* that brings ultimate satisfaction and fulfillment. We must take the "above the sun" approach to our work. If we do not, the end result will be emptiness.

Now examine verses 8-11.

What two things are never satisfied according to verse 8?

I live this everyday. As I click on facebook and scroll down, then twitter and scroll down, then Youtube and scroll down, and then Instagram and scroll down. There is always something more to see or listen to. I could scroll all day long if I wanted to and never tire of what I'm seeing and hearing. The same goes for the remote control with the television. We could flip from channel to channel all day long but never be satisfied. We will still desire a new experience and keep searching for one.

What does Solomon conclude in verses 9-11?

Advertisers are always trying to sell us new and improved products. They know that buyers grow dissatisfied easily and they play on that innate need for something new.

And is it really true there is "nothing new under the sun"? What about all this technology?

Consider...light bulbs resemble the sun, motorcycles resemble horses, airplanes resemble birds and computers resemble our brains! All the modern discoveries and inventions hinge on the creativity of our God. We hear of people saying the world seems more violent and sinful today than ever before. But consider, Cain killed Abel back in Genesis 4. Murder has been with us since the beginning of time.

And finally, in verse 11, what do we see Solomon grappling with?

Do you remember your great grandparents? How about your great great great grandparents? As generations come and go, we forget who came before us. God will use each of us in our own sphere of influence for His glory but may we never seek to make a difference for our own glory because at the end of the day, there is no glory for man, the idea of fame is a mirage. We must not be deceived into chasing after it.

Thankfully, our faith in God changes everything. There is something "new" under the sun, because God is ruling over the sun! Jesus Christ, the Son of God, ushered in the New Covenant in His blood at the cross (Luke 22:20). Those of us who believe become "new" creations in Christ Jesus (2 Corinthians 5:17).

Thank you Jesus for our salvation. Thank you for giving me a "new" heart and a "new" spirit! (Ezekiel 36:26)

Verse of the Day:

Satisfy us in the morning

with your steadfast love,

so that we may rejoice

and be glad

all of our days.

Psalm 90:14

Day Two—The Vanity of Wisdom
Ecclesiastes 1: 12-18

Let's begin with prayer.

Slowly read or color-code Ecclesiastes 1:12-18. (I used a mix of orange, blue, gray and purple.)

Remember, there is no right or wrong way to do the coloring. It is simply a tool to help us slow down and soak in every Word of God.

I remember my senior year of public high school, all I could dream of was getting out of that place and off to college at the Moody Bible Institute. I was sure that Bible School would be a utopia of sorts, where everyone got along and sang Kum Ba Ya all day long. I was wrong.

I loved my studies, professors and friends but I discovered that not everyone was there for the studies. Some were sent there, by their parents, some were there to find a mate and others had a rebellious spirit.

Many go off to college with rose-colored glasses imagining that this is where they are going to "find" themselves and find fulfillment in life. But instead of finding those things— they find alcoholism, broken relationships, humanism, disgruntled faculty workers, political activism, controversy, loads of coffee, stress and even failure sometimes.

As we are about to see, intellectual pursuits apart from God are just another dead end road of painful dissatisfaction.

We already know from our first week of study that Solomon's wisdom exceeded that of any man who lived before or after him. How do we know from verse 14 that Solomon is seeking for human wisdom, apart from God?

Solomon is only looking at a man's life from an earthly perspective. As a believer, our education should have one goal...to glorify God.

Why do you think he calls our work under heaven an "unhappy business"?

Life is hard living under the curse of the Garden of Eden. We live in a fallen world.

As king, Solomon would have had an Ivy League sort of education. It would have been the best of the best. He would have studied science, history, philosophy, literature, ethics, and fine arts.

But when he examines life, what does he conclude in verse 15.

Verse 15 is considered a proverb. A proverb is a short pithy saying stating a general truth.

How many times have I read blog posts and articles and books where authors write—"we can change the world!" It seems to be the mantra of our generation and while I do believe we all play a role in God's changing of this world, may we never forget, we do not have the power to change anything through our own human efforts. Man cannot fix this world.

I've seen youth jaded when they realize the futility of trying to change the world because the world is extremely crooked and cannot be made straight.

But God is at work. He is redeeming and changing lives. He is setting captives free. He is giving hope to the hopeless. He is giving victory to the defeated. He is giving new life in dead places and one day He will take us to be with Him forever in a perfect place! Our hope is not in education and is not found under the sun but above it!

Read verses 16 & 17. Solomon not only searched out wisdom and knowledge but what else did he seek to know in verse 17?

Why do you think he wanted to know about this?

Verse 17 could be a reference to Solomon's falling away from God into disobedience and even idolatry (I Kings 11:1-9). Did he find joy in madness and folly?

Sometimes the more we try to know and understand the meaning of life, the more frustrated we can become by life's unanswerable questions. Solomon seems to conclude that human wisdom is useless and only brings us great pain and sorrow

"Set your minds on things that are above, not on things that are on earth."
Colossians 3:2

Solomon's mind was set on the temporary things of this earth. Nothing satisfied him.

Psalm 90:14 says what will satisfy and bring joy to our lives. The verse is a part of a prayer of Moses to our great God.

"Satisfy us in the morning with your steadfast love, so that we
may rejoice and be glad all of our days."

May we begin our day with this same prayer, that God would satisfy the longings of our heart with His steadfast love. When we know the satisfaction of God's great love for us, our pain and sorrow "under the sun" turns to an overflowing gladness of the Lord!

DISCUSSION QUESTIONS:

What lessons have you learned so far about the meaning of work, knowledge and wisdom?

How are you living? Are you living only for this world, "under the sun" and "chasing after the wind," or are you living for Jesus, who is the Creator of the sun and is above the sun?

Let's pray.

Thank you Lord for your steadfast love that never fails. Help us to daily seek your wisdom in your Word. Help us to serve and work for your glory and not our own. Give us joy on our journey of life. In Jesus' great name we pray, amen.

Verse of the Day:

Whatever you do, work heartily,

as for the Lord and not for men.

Colossians 3:23

Day Three—The Vanity of Pleasure
Ecclesiastes 2: 1-11

Let's begin with prayer.

Slowly read or color-code Ecclesiastes 2:1-11. (I used a lot of gray today.)

Have you ever noticed how life's pleasures are brief? A few summers ago, my daughter received a butterfly net. She chased butterflies for many days before catching one. Then she caught one and as she went to examine it—-out it flew! She was so disappointed.

Pleasure is the same way. We can't put it in a bottle and keep it. All great evenings and weekends and vacations come to an end and we are left with our own reality. By nature, we are all pleasure seekers. We are always seeking to feel good. Sometimes that means we look for it in relationships, other times in food or drink, clothes, projects, houses, cars, entertainment and laughter.

In Ecclesiastes 2, Solomon begins with himself as he searches for meaning. Over and over in this passage he says "I", "my", "me", or "myself." He didn't look for an older mentor, or to his father David or even to God for the answers. He decided he'd figure this one out on his own.

According to verses 1 & 2, where does he start his search?

Don't we all enjoy a good clean comedian, sit-com or movie? Proverbs 14:13 tells us, *"Even in laughter the heart may ache."*

What does Solomon turn to next according to verse 3?

Ephesians 5:18 tells us, we are not to get drunk with wine. Solomon does not abandon himself to drunkenness but rather to the experience of fine wine. He lets his elegant taste lead but again, he finds a dead end road. So he rolls up his sleeves and gets to work.

DISCUSSION QUESTION:

Before we look at his projects, let's pause and reflect. What messages have we received from the world regarding pleasure, laughter and wine? Tell about a time when seeking after one of these three things led you to a dead end road.

Solomon also mentions that he explored folly. We all know of fools who seem to be much happier than those who are prudent. So Solomon is leaving no stone unturned.

Read verses 4-8. What does Solomon focus on accumulating?

Solomon attempted to build heaven on earth.

When my Great Uncle died, our family gathered at his home to clean it out. A dumpster was placed in the driveway for all of the things that were worn out or useless. We stacked it full. A lifetime of hard work and toil went straight to the dumpster.

In Luke 12:15, Jesus warns: *"Take care, and be on your guard against all covetousness, for one's life does not consist in the abundance of his possessions."*

Have you looked at someone else's home or abundance of possessions and been jealous of it. Don't be. As we have seen by many famous singers and actors who have committed suicide, these things are a mirage. They do not lead to peace and happiness.

Also, consider for a moment all of these concubines Solomon had. I Kings 11:3 tells us he had 700 wives and 300 concubines. That's enough for him to have a woman any time of day to meet all of his sensual needs. But surely along with these women came jealousy, gossiping, infighting and strife.

Sadly, many today have fallen into the trap of pornography. They can access it any time of day to meet all of their sensual needs but they've been sold a lie. It's an empty, futile lie that will eat away at their life like cancer.

What does Solomon conclude about his projects and possessions according to verses 9-11?

Solomon denied himself nothing and he took pleasure in his toil.

Colossians 3:23 tells us, *"Whatever you do, work heartily, as for the Lord and not for men."*

It is not wrong to find pleasure in our work. The famous Olympic runner Eric Liddell once said, *"God made me fast. And when I run I feel His pleasure."*

When our projects and dreams and goals are what God created us to do, and we do them for the Lord, there is pleasure. Solomon did not do these for the Lord, he did them for himself. Selfish endeavors lead to a meaningless existence and unsatisfied longings.

What do these verses tell us about our pleasures and earthly treasures?

Matthew 6:19-21

2 Timothy 3:1-5

We weren't made to find pleasure in the gifts God gives us but rather in the giver of the gifts.

In verse 11, Solomon "considered" all his hands had done. In the Hebrew, "considered" means to literally face something or someone and look it straight in the eye.

Pause for a moment and look your life straight in the eye. What gifts has God given you that you need to stop using for your own purposes and begin using for His glory? (it may be a dream, a possession, a position or something else God is laying on your heart right now.)

Let's Pray.

Dear Heavenly Father, please reveal to us the things in our life that we have selfishly pursued. Turn them into gifts that we use for your glory. Help us to walk in the truth we have learned today. In Jesus' great name we pray, amen.

Verse of the Day:

Let us not grow weary

of doing good,

for in due season we will reap,

if we do not give up.

Galatians 6:9

Day Four—Comparing Wisdom and Folly
Ecclesiastes 2: 12-17

Let's begin with prayer.

Slowly read or color-code Ecclesiastes 2:12-17. (Mine is mostly blue, gray and purple.)

There was a time when my ministry had around 40,000 followers on Facebook. Then in a matter of a few short months, it shot up to around 140,000 followers and I was thrilled. Then Facebook changed their algorithm causing many of the business and ministry pages to get hidden from our follower's feed. I became frantic and Googled how to fix this, only to discover there was no way to change what Facebook was automatically doing. Suddenly the number 140,000 was meaningless. Who cared if I had 140,000 followers if only 500 could see my posts? So what if my work there was done with great care to bless the followers if they weren't seeing it? For months, this annoyed me, then I had a big "come to Jesus" moment where I had to let it go and trust it into God's hands.

In verse 12 we see that Solomon takes a new turn. Now he is considering the comparison between wisdom and folly.

Which does he decide is better according to verse 13?

What fate awaits both of them?

Death is certain and universal. No matter how wise or foolish, how wealthy, or hardworking, statistics show one out of one --die.

Look up Psalm 49:10. What does it say about the death of the wise and the fool?

What also bothers Solomon about their same fate according to verse 16?

Remembrance and fame is another mirage. The Internet has made it possible for a penniless young girl to sing a song in her bedroom, record it and become famous. The dream for many is to go from rags to riches. But when their 15 minutes of fame is up, some drop into deep depression because they have been forgotten and replaced with the new "It" girl.

Selfies abound on the Internet as kids strike a pose and take photos of themselves, as if they are models. Their hope is that people will give them attention and tell them they are pretty. They find their significance in being seen.

Worrying about what others remember about us, is a trap. When we are rejected and forgotten, pushed aside for a job promotion or a new friend, we realize we are feeding a needy beast that is never full.

We honor our dead with tombstones made of marble and granite in hopes that their names do not wear off in the sunshine and rain. We don't want to be forgotten. But within a generation or two the reality is, most of us are forgotten. Even in Egypt where huge pyramids were built as tombs to remember their Pharaohs, very few of us can name those Pharaohs.

What does Solomon conclude in verse 17?

Solomon is at another dead end. He hates life. Now before we all fall into a deep pit of depression as we realize the futility of so much of our lives, let's remember that Solomon is assessing life without God.

As believers, how should we view death and/or labor according to these passages?

I Corinthians 15:55-58

Philippians 2:12-16

Galatians 6:6-10

Galatians 6:9 is my life verse. It is a verse that has kept me going when it seemed like my labor and work for the Lord was in vain. It has kept me going when it seemed like my spiritual training of my children was not bearing fruit. It has kept me doing good to my husband, in the midst of dry spells in our marriage.

DISCUSSION QUESTION:

How does Galatians 6:9 encourage you in the midst of the season of life you are in today?

Dear readers, do not give up. Be assured, your labor for the Lord is not in vain. Keep going!

Verse of the Day:

To the one who pleases Him,

God has given wisdom

and knowledge and joy.

Ecclesiastes 2:26

Day Five—The Vanity of Work
Eccesiastes 2: 18-26

Let's begin with prayer.

Slowly read or color-code Ecclesiastes 2:18-26. (Mine is a mix of blue, gray, purple and green.)

Solomon was the king of Israel, and God had blessed him with great wealth. However, Solomon realized that he could not take it with him when he died.

Jesus told a similar parable in Luke 12:16-21 about a rich man who tore down his barns in order to build bigger barns in which to store all his crops and goods. This man told himself that now he could take it easy and eat, drink and be merry. God said this man was a fool because that night his soul would be required of him, and he would die. All of his goods were then given to someone else. This man had laid up treasure for himself, but was not rich towards God.

This is true for all who have stored up treasures on this earth. Everything we have worked for and accumulated will be left behind when we die. It's possible that our heirs will foolishly waste our hard-earned wealth, but once we are gone from this earth, they will become the "master" of all that we have worked for under the sun. We will no longer have any control over it.

In verse 18, we see that Solomon hated something. What did he hate and why?

Verse 20 says that after Solomon considered this, his heart was in despair and depressed.

When we meet someone, we often introduce ourselves by saying, "I am a teacher, author, doctor, mother, or librarian." We are defined by our work. Some people become workaholics thinking this will give their lives more meaning while others are lazy slackers. Either way, work leaves us empty on the inside.

According to verse 23, what happens at night to the workaholic and how long does this last?

DISCUSSION QUESTION:

Have you experienced this in life? You commit to something that looks enjoyable but later you find it steals your sleep and your peace and you regret ever saying yes? Tell about this time and what you learned?

Finally, Solomon brings God into the picture! What do verses 24-26 say about Solomon's solution to his problems?

Oh friends, I love this conclusion. Do you see this nugget of wisdom tucked so tightly in here?

It's the simple things. Eating, drinking and working, those come from the hand of God. These are good things. These are daily mercies that should bring us pleasure. We do not have to go chasing every rainbow! We can come around the dinner table with family or friends and be refreshed. We can relax in the evening after a hard day of honest work and be content. Enjoyment comes from the hand of God.

According to verse 26, God has given His children wisdom, knowledge and joy. It is the unsaved sinner who has to toil and be about the business of collecting and gathering. That is not our business—that is vanity!

Like Solomon, have you confronted your own mortality? Will you be remembered as one who gathered and collected or as one who was content with the simple pleasures of life that come from the hand of God? What will be your legacy?

Thank you for a great week of study! Let's close in prayer.

Dear Heavenly Father,

Thank you for the simple pleasures of life that come from your hand as food and drink. God, you are good and in your hand are wisdom and joy. Help us to use our talents, time and hard work for your glory. Give us a sweet night of rest tonight. In Jesus' name I pray, Amen.

Week 3~Ecclesiastes 3 & 4

Verse of the Day:

He has made everything

beautiful in its time.

Ecclesiastes 3:11

Day One—A Time for Everything
Ecclesiastes 3: 1-8

Let's begin with prayer.

Slowly read or color-code Ecclesiastes 3:1-8.

Change. Do you like it? I suppose it matters if it's a good change or a bad change. Is it a pay raise or a job loss? Is it a newborn baby or the death of a loved one?

Ecclesiastes 3 describes 28 different seasons of life and one thing is guaranteed... change. Change is absolute.

In John 14, when Jesus met with His disciples He told them change was coming. He was going to depart but they were to have no fear because he was sending them the Holy Spirit.

The Greek word for "Holy Spirit" is "parakletos" which means: *one who comes along side and helps and comforts.*

God uses change to shape us and to open our eyes to His presence. We are not alone. We need to learn to embrace change. This is easier to write than to do. But change is what turned Mary the peasant girl into the mother of God Almighty! Change is what turned David the shepherd boy into the King of Israel! And the change of Jesus' blood covering over our sins is what turns you and me from sinners to saints!

Let's examine these 28 seasons or times of life that Solomon writes about.

Time is a key word in this chapter. Webster's Dictionary says time is a period between two events or a measurable interval.

What are the times that Solomon speaks of in verse 2?

God is sovereign. He determines the day we will be born and the day we will die.

What do these verses say about our number of days?

Psalm 139:13-16

Matthew 6:27

Psalm 31:15

     Verse 2 also speaks of planting and plucking. Farmers sow seeds and harvest their crop at appointed times each year. To sow is the farmer's responsibility but the water, sunshine, seasons and cycles of nature come from the hand of God. God is sovereign over all.

What times do verses 3 and 4 speak of?

     We see that God is in the midst of our relationships and our emotional responses to the changes of life.

Now examine verses 5-8. List the times Solomon speaks of.

Sometimes we are tempted to think that we are the only ones experiencing the joys or pains of life. Do you see from this list that seasons of life are normal? There is order to our lives. Some are pleasurable and some are painful. There are positive things and negative things that happen to all of us. Life "under heaven" runs this way.

Which of these 28 seasons are you in the midst of today? How have you seen God in this season of life?

Perhaps you are mourning the loss of a loved one or celebrating the marriage of a child. Perhaps you have just made a new friend or you have just said goodbye as you moved to a new town. Perhaps you lost something and have been looking for it and are not giving up your search. Or perhaps you have given up and are letting it go. Perhaps you have cleaned out your kitchen and thrown things away or you are in the midst of remodeling your kitchen. Perhaps you confronted a friend and it did not go well and now it's time to be silent.

For every positive there is a negative. The sum total is zero. So at the end of it all Solomon is befuddled. Tomorrow we will look at how Solomon reacts to his reflections.

In conclusion, let's consider our use of time. We use watches, clocks, phones and calendars to order our lives. We all have the same amount of time each day, 24 hours. No matter your status in life, no one has more or less time than another.

DISCUSSION QUESTION:

Read Ephesians 5:15-16 and Psalm 90:12. What are we to use to guide how we use our time? How do these apply to your season of life today?

How we use our time does matter to God. Let's close in prayer, asking God to direct us wisely as we fill our calendars each day.

Verse of the Day:

For we are his workmanship,

created in Christ Jesus

for good works,

which God prepared beforehand.

Ephesians 2:10

Day Two—He Makes All Things Beautiful
Ecclesiastes 3: 9-15

Let's begin with prayer.

Slowly read or color-code Ecclesiastes 3:9-15.

Read verses 9 and 10. According to verse 11. What has God made with time?

How is man's perspective of time different from God's perspective of time?

When we pour out a puzzle from a box and begin to put it together, at first it is a mess. Then one corner is complete and that part is pleasing to the eye. Then other pieces begin to fit together. At times, I have to walk away from a large puzzle and come back to it because it frustrates me. A little perspective makes it more manageable. But after time passes and the picture is complete, it is beautiful.

All of our lives are like puzzles. God has brought each piece together. He uses the good and the bad to shape us and show himself faithful. He uses our trials and triumphs to draw us to Him and reveal Himself. We must be patient with God as He writes our story and makes everything beautiful in its time.

DISCUSSION QUESTION:
Share something in your life that God has made beautiful through time.

How do we become aware of eternity according to verse 11?

There is a consciousness in all of us that senses there is more to life than just the here and now. We see this in little girls who dress up as princesses and dream of being a part of another kingdom.

This world is like Cinderella's Ball. The greatest day or joy eventually comes to an end. The clock strikes midnight and we fall on hard times. All joys we have here on earth are just a taste of what is coming in heaven. The Magic Kingdom of Disney World pales in comparison to the kingdom of heaven where the clock will never strike midnight again. Forever we will be with the King of Kings and there we will live in joy for eternity!

God put a curiosity for eternity within us even as little children, so we would seek after Him. Yet according to verse 11, we cannot see the "big picture". We cannot see from beginning to the end but someday we will!

What does Solomon conclude in verses 12 & 13?

God grants the believer the ability to have joy and do good. He also gives good gifts of food, drink and work.

I have been on missions trips and seen believers around the world singing to the Lord in shanties. We Americans marvel at their ability to have joy and do good to others, when they have so very little. Perhaps they have discovered that the gift of food, drink and work is enough and it is we who feel the need to keep running after every pipe dream. We are the ones lacking in joy and the time to do good to others.

How are you practicing the pleasure of food, drink and work in your life? Is there anything you need to change?

Read Ephesians 2:10. As believers, what are we to be doing?

And finally, what do verses 14 & 15 teach us about God?

Recently, I was sitting at a pool with friends talking about a trial in my life. I was surprised and comforted to discover that both of my friends had experienced the exact same problem! Verse 15 tells us that life continuously replays itself. Things I'm facing, most likely you are facing as well. Our lives are a replay of each other. Do you fight with your husband? Me too. Do you struggle with losing your temper with your children? Me too. Are you tired of the piles of laundry? Me too!

Social media has shown me that we all are living parallel lives. Our struggles and difficulties are common. Sometimes we feel alone, like we are the only ones facing certain trials, but this is not the case. Many are struggling today around the world with the same things you are struggling with. Sometimes God will replay trials in our life over and over until we learn our lesson well. God is patient like that. He goes the distance with us.

Is there something reoccurring in your life that has your attention. What could God be teaching you through this?

Close in prayer by praying about this situation and handing it over to God.

Verse of the Day:

Our citizenship is in heaven,

and from it we await a Savior,

the Lord Jesus Christ.

Philippians 3:20

Day Three—Injustice and Death
Ecclesiastes 3: 16-22

Let's begin with prayer.

Slowly read or color-code Ecclesiastes 3:16-22.

Each of us has a sense of justice and fairness within us. Even small children will say, "that's not fair" when a sibling gets a larger portion of ice cream in his bowl!

When we see a loved one suffering heartache, we feel sad. But when we see a loved one suffering under injustice, we feel mad.

Read verses 16 and 17. What does Solomon say exists alongside justice and righteousness?

Even though man's system of justice may fail, what does Solomon know about God's divine judgment that gives comfort and peace in our circumstances?

Read 2 Corinthians 5:10 and Romans 12:19. What does it say about God's judgment?

God's judgment is not often immediate, but a final Day of Judgment is coming for all mankind. God's justice will prevail, but we must wait for it.

Recently a believer hurt me deeply. I know this person will be forever with me in heaven and may never suffer consequences from their injustice against me. I also know that God has called me to forgive this person. But what I had to learn in order to forgive is that God already paid the consequences for their injustice. He was nailed to the cross for the sins of this person, as well as my sins. The debt for this sin has been paid in full. Each time the situation came to mind, I had to take my thoughts captive and go directly to the cross with it—remembering that Jesus took it upon himself to make this wrong right. Let's not take revenge, grow bitter or hold grudges but leave our hurts at the foot of the cross.

Now read verses 18-21. What does Solomon say is the destiny of all flesh, man and beast?

Are man and animals the same? Do we have superiority over them? What is in our hearts that is not in an animal's heart according to Ecclesiastes 3:11?

In this passage we see human questioning not doctrinal fact. What do the passages below say about the spirit and soul of a believer at the time of death?

2 Corinthians 5:8

Philippians 3:20-21

Eternity is in God's hands and something we will all experience! Solomon concludes in verse 22, that we must rejoice in our work and our lot in life.

DISCUSSION QUESTION:

What is your lot or portion in life? What work has God called you to, in this season of life? How can you experience more joy in the present?

Little girls dream of prince charming whisking them away, on a white horse, to live happily ever. Dreams do come true! Read Revelation 19 below.

11 Then I saw heaven opened, and behold, a white horse! The one sitting on it is called Faithful and True, and in righteousness he judges and makes war. 12 His eyes are like a flame of fire, and on his head are many diadems, and he has a name written that no one knows but himself. 13 He is clothed in a robe dipped in blood, and the name by which he is called is The Word of God. 14 And the armies of heaven, arrayed in fine linen, white and pure, were following him on white horses. 15 From his mouth comes a sharp sword with which to strike down the nations, and he will rule them with a rod of iron. He will tread the winepress of the fury of the wrath of God the Almighty. 16 On his robe and on his thigh he has a name written, King of kings and Lord of lords.

If this world has dealt you a royally bad hand, hang on, it won't be long now until you stand face to face with the King of Kings! Take hope and courage from this truth and live with defiant joy. He loves you so.

Verse of the Day:

Better is a handful of quietness

than two hands full of toil

and a striving after wind.

Ecclesiastes 4:6

Day Four—Affliction and Competition
Ecclesiastes 4: 1-8

Let's begin with prayer.

Slowly read or color-code Ecclesiastes 4:1-8.

While Solomon explores riches and wisdom and living the high life, he also explores the depths of pain and suffering that people face, under the sun.

Solomon is discouraged by the oppression of this world. What does he conclude in verses 1-3?

As Christians, what should be our response to oppression in this world?

Read 2 Corinthians 1:3-4. How does God use our afflictions in the lives of others?

In verses 4 and 5 we see two contrasts of living. First, we see in verse 4, the successful and skilled person. This person has made it to the top through comparing and competing with their peers. The drive to be number one and the envy of anyone better than them, has made them more skilled.

The last of the 10 commandments in Exodus 20:17 says, you shall not covet your neighbor's house, wife, servants, animals or anything your neighbor has. This is a sinful way of living and it displeases God.

Next we see in verse 5, the lazy person with no ambition or direction in life. He will end up with nothing. 2 Thessalonians 3:10b says, "if anyone is not willing to work, let him not eat." Laziness is a sinful way of living and it displeases God as well.

In verse 6, what does Solomon say is a better path to follow?

It is so very hard for mothers today to slow down. The world tells us to move it! Get those kids signed up for soccer, piano, gymnastics, basketball, football, baseball—you name it, it feels like everybody's doing it!

The world tells us to get our calendars full and stay on the move. If you don't, your kids might miss out or they won't be cool or they won't learn important life lessons. Competition keeps moms filling their calendars out of fear.

But verse 6 shows us that there is value in quietness. This world does not know the rest that our savior Jesus offers. They don't have to run all over God's green earth to find meaning; they simply have to run into the arms of the maker of the earth.

What do these verses say about quietness and rest?

Matthew 11:28

I Timothy 6:6

Proverbs 15:16

DISCUSSION QUESTION:

As you examine your own life, how are you doing with balancing work and rest? Are you living a one-handful or two-handful style of life?

Finally, in verse 8 we see the workaholic loner. "His eyes are never satisfied with riches" and he never questions why he is working himself so hard. This is vanity.

Let's just pause in the middle of our striving and ask ourselves why. Why do we do the things we do? If we aren't satisfied today, what makes us believe we will be satisfied tomorrow? Let's face it. Nothing here on earth will ever fully satisfy us. We must stop following the ways of the world and instead walk in the ways of the Word.

Is there something in your hand that you need to put down to find rest? Give it to God in prayer right now.

Verse of the Day:

Two are better than one,

Because they have a good reward for their toil.

For if they fall, one will lift up his fellow,

But woe to him who is alone when he falls

and has not another to lift him up!

Ecclesiastes 4:9,10

Day Five—Friendships and a Fickle Crowd
Ecclesiastes 4: 9-16

Let's begin with prayer.

Slowly read or color-code Ecclesiastes 4:9-16.

Women friendships. They can be complicated. We all know how hard friendships are for little girls. There are mean girls and cliques and teasing and gossip. Then we grow into big girls and hopefully by this point we have learned a few things about how to be a good friend and how to avoid the "porcupine" people who poke at us.

God created women, with the need for relationships. List the characteristics of a true friend in the following verses:

Verse 9

Verse 10

Verse 11

Verse 12

What does Solomon conclude is even better than two people partnered together in verse 12?

Imagine one uncooked spaghetti noodle. It is easy to snap right in half. Now imagine a bundle of spaghetti noodles. They are much harder to break when they are all together. In the same way, when we have a cord of three strands including God on our side, we are stronger.

God has designed us to live in relationship with Him and with others. We were never meant to live alone, but to share our life with others. This is especially true of Christians because we need the close fellowship and support of other believers.

DISCUSSION QUESTION:

Who are some of the friends that God has placed in your life that you support, love and protect, and who does this for you?

We see in scripture close friends like Moses and Aaron, David and Jonathon, Ruth and Naomi, Paul and Barnabas and Paul and Timothy. If you do not have a dear friend like this, remember, Jesus is the best friend of all!

Jesus says in John 15:5, "No longer do I call you servants, for the servant does not know what the master is doing; but I have called you friends, for all that I have heard from my Father I have made known to you."

Have you made Jesus your friend?

Praise and thank God for His friendship. He is always with you.

Consider how you can be a better friend to the women God has placed into your life.

Observe verses 13-16.

Solomon concludes this chapter with a warning to leaders. These principles apply to any sort of leader.

What did you learn about the disadvantages and advantages of the poor wise youth and the king?

The youth was born in poverty but with wisdom. He was a commoner and for some reason had been in prison, whether justly or unjustly. The old King had ruled so long that pride turned him into a fool who would not listen to wise counsel.

Because the youth possessed wisdom and the king was foolish, what was the youth able to do?

What eventually happened to the public support of the young king?

Solomon concludes this too is vanity and a striving after the wind.

Crowds are fickle. Popularity is fleeting. May we never believe that admiration or fame replaces genuine, loyal friendships.

We saw this in Matthew 21 when Jesus rode into Jerusalem on a donkey. He received a reception of praise from the people as they spread their cloaks and tree branches on the road and shouted, "Hosanna in the Highest!" The people acknowledged Jesus as their King. But one week later, the very same people were rejecting Jesus and demanding His death by crucifixion. (Matthew 27:15-23)

If this happened to Jesus, it can happen to any leader. However, we know the end of the story. After His death on the cross and burial, Jesus Christ rose from the grave. Later He ascended into heaven. He has promised to return to this earth again. This time, He will not be rejected, but He will rule and reign as the King of Kings and Lord of Lords forever!

Praise His name forever!

Week 4~Ecclesiastes 5, 6 & 7

Verse of the Day:

No one can serve two masters, for

either he will hate the one

and love the other, or he

will be devoted to the one

and despise the other.

You cannot serve God and money.

Matthew 6:24

Day One—Dreaming To the Glory of God
Ecclesiastes 5: 1-7

Let's begin with prayer.

Slowly read or color-code Ecclesiastes 5:1-7.

By nature, man is instinctively religious. We long to worship something. But some have turned religion into a charade where they attend church on Sundays, say prayers and make vows but live contrary to God's word the other 6 days of the week.

Before entering the house of God, how do you prepare yourself for corporate worship?

Hebrews 10:24-25 says: *"And let us consider how to stir up one another to love and good works, not neglecting to meet together, as is the habit of some, but encouraging one another, and all the more as you see the Day drawing near."*

We are commanded as believers to come together. It is not optional but the manner in which we come matters as well.

What strong warning does Solomon give in verse 1?

Solomon cautions the way we approach God and the way we speak to God. What did you learn about the use of your words when speaking to God in prayer in verses 2 & 3?

What does Proverbs 29:20 say about a man who is reckless with his words?

Speaking slowly, carefully, thoughtfully and sincerely to God is an indication of wisdom.

In the Sermon on the Mount in Matthew 6:7, Jesus taught, *"and when you pray, do not heap up empty phrases as the Gentiles do, for they think they will be heard for their many words."* God is not impressed by our many words when we pray!

In verses 4-7, we are cautioned when making vows to God. How does Solomon say we should make them?

In Hebrew the word "vow" is "nedar" which means to promise, to do or give something to God.

What are some examples of vows or promises you have voluntarily made to God?

In verse 6 we see an excuse made for breaking the vow. What is a common excuse? And how does God respond to our broken vows?

Whenever a messenger of God or a priest from the Temple came to collect on a vow that had been made (possibly a financial promise or gift), the individual wanted to be free of their promise to God.

When vows are made, to the best of our ability, they should be kept. This includes marriage vows.

Twice in this passage the words "dream" and "dreams" are mentioned (v3, 7). What is the warning for dreams?

"God is the one we must fear." (v.7)

We live in a world where the mantra to our children is "dream big". If they can imagine it, they can do it. Ecclesiastes tells us, dreams come with much business and vanity. To put it another way, dreams come with a lot of hard work and sometimes that hard work becomes vanity when it is outside the will of God.

We must lay every dream before God's throne in prayer and wait and listen and seek God's will for our lives.

DISCUSSION QUESTION:

Do you have a dream? What is it? Have you asked God what His will is for that dream?

As verse 2 says, *"God is in heaven and you are on earth."* His ways are higher than ours. We must not be hasty following every whim we can imagine and making vows to God. Sometimes in the midst of our dreams, we are tempted to vow to God that a certain percentage of what we make will go to feed the hungry or to build an orphanage. Then all too often, the money comes in and the vow to give back to God, is broken.

Let's not be hasty. Let's keep our promises to God. Pray now and give your dreams to the Lord for His glory.

Verse of the Day:

For the love of money

is a root of all kinds of evils.

It is through this craving that some

have wandered away from the faith

and pierced themselves with many pangs.

1 Timothy 6:10

Day Two—Enjoying the Simple Things
Ecclesiastes 5: 8-20

Let's begin with prayer.

Slowly read or color-code Ecclesiastes 5:8-20.

As we begin our study in the second half of chapter 5, we see the inevitability of the oppression of the poor and injustice. Solomon says to not be amazed or surprised.

Then Solomon returns to the main topic of chapter 2, on the meaninglessness of personal wealth and riches. We will see that money can buy many things but it can't buy contentment.

What does Solomon state in verse 10 about one who loves money?

Notice, Solomon is not speaking about one who merely possesses money, but one who loves money.

What do these two passages say about the love of money:

Matthew 6:24

1 Timothy 6:10

What additional problem does Solomon point out in verse 11?

The more we have, the less we can use what we have. I'll admit, I have a closet full of clothes. Each time I gain weight, I save the smaller sizes in case I lose weight and fit into them again. At this point, I have some clothes that have been waiting on me for years to lose weight. What good are they to me? I can see them with my eyes but I cannot wear them.

What irony is contrasted in verse 12?

In verse 13, what do earthly riches bring to the one who hoards them up?

Have you ever watched the television show "Hoarders"? It is horrifying to see inside the house of a person who has held onto useless possessions, even junk and garbage. Their hoarding has ruined not only their own life but the lives of those who love them. Holding onto useless possessions often destroys lives. There is no pleasure or joy in hoarding.

Free yourself today from a place in your home where you have been hoarding things you have not used in years. Perhaps there's a drawer, closet, cabinet, basement or garage that needs cleaned out. Do it. You will feel so much better!

In verses 13-17, we see a man who worked hard, hoarded his riches and lost it all. What happened to him?

According to Jesus in Matthew 6:19-21, where should we be storing up treasures?

This chapter closes with comforting words.

We see in verse 18 that it is good and fitting to eat, drink and find enjoyment in all the work we do. We should accept this as our lot in life.

DISCUSSION QUESTIONS:

What gifts are stated in verse 18-20 that God has given us?

Do you enjoy these simple things in life? Why or why not?

Does prosperity guarantee a happy, satisfied life?

Let's choose contentment today. Close in prayer and ask God to help you live a life of contentment and joy found only in Him.

Verse of the Day:

Jesus said to them,

"I am the bread of life; whoever comes

to me shall not hunger,

and whoever believes in me

shall never thirst.

John 6:35

Day Three—Craving More
Ecclesiastes 6: 1-12

Begin with prayer.

Slowly read or color-code Ecclesiastes 6:1-12

We closed yesterday's study, remembering that true joy and contentment is a gift from God. Now Solomon returns back to the subject of the vanity of wealth. Perhaps this is a lesson we need to read and meditate on multiple times to truly grasp. So, let's dive in!

In verses 1 & 2, what is a grievous evil?

Have you seen this? Perhaps someone works hard all of their life but then has failing health right in the prime of their life. The second house they thought they would enjoy in their golden years may end up rented out to strangers for their enjoyment.

In verses 3-6, what exaggerated terminology is used to describe the size of this man's family and the length of his time on this earth?

What part of him is not satisfied with life's good things?

God had greatly blessed this man with a long life, large family, and all of life's good things, but this man found no satisfaction or joy in his soul. Without God in his life, he was spiritually bankrupt. As Solomon has said over and over, it is "vanity". A life lived apart from God brings no lasting joy or satisfaction. It is meaningless.

Read verses 7-9. What statement does Solomon make in verse 7 about man's mouth?

Whether you are the President of a huge company eating steak dinners or a college student working part-time to eat hamburgers, we all work for one thing—food. It's amazing how our appetite for food drives us. We can eat a massive breakfast and be stuffed to the gills and by lunch be hungry all over again! Our hunger drives us.

Wealth is the same. It never satisfies. We always have a craving for more. No matter what material thing you choose to fill your void in your soul with, it will be lacking.

When my children were young they begged for Happy Meals. They loved the toy inside. But the "happy meal" only made them "happy" for about 30 minutes and so the next day they would beg again for a "happy meal." As adults, our "happy meals" just grow bigger and more expensive. We continue to need a nice dinner out, new clothing, new cars or new houses. We are content for a few weeks and then we need more.

In verse 9, what does Solomon say is better than "the wandering of the appetite?"

It is better to be content and satisfied with what your eyes see today, with the things you presently have, than to dream about and long for things you do not have but hope to have in the future.

Turn to John 6:35. How does Jesus satisfy our appetites?

Sweet Jesus. Only in Him will we be fully satisfied.

Now read verses 10-12 as this chapter concludes, bringing us to the midpoint of the book of Ecclesiastes.

Solomon asks two questions in verse 12. The first is: "Who knows what is good for a man?" How would you answer this for Solomon?

The second question is: "Who can tell a man what will be after him?" How would you answer this?

God knows! God has foreordained our lives and has a plan and a purpose for each one of us. We are to learn to be content with whatever He gives us, finding our joy and satisfaction in Him.

Our future life depends upon what we have done with Jesus in this present earthly life lived "under the sun." Do we believe in Jesus as the Son of God, crucified, risen and coming again? Do we agree we are sinners and have we repented of our sins?

1 John 1:9 says: *"If we confess our sins, he is faithful and just to forgive us our sins and to cleanse us from all unrighteousness."*

If you have done this, then you can know that you will live for eternity in the presence of the Lord. That is your future destiny!

DISCUSSION QUESTION:

Are the people around you "happy"? What do you see the world chasing after? Has any of their thinking crept into yours and in what ways?

If we live our life without God, it will not matter the size of our bank account, the number of our children or the length of days we live. A life lived without God is vanity but a life lived for God's glory will bring lasting joy and meaning. Let's choose joy today!

Verse of the Day:

I have fought the good fight,

I have finished the race,

I have kept the faith.

2 Timothy 4:7

Day Four—Ending Well
Ecclesiastes 7: 1-13

Begin with prayer.

Slowly read or color-code Ecclesiastes 7:1-13.

When you think of these names what comes to mind?

> Mary Mother of Jesus
>
> Hillary
>
> Taylor
>
> Beth
>
> Kim
>
> Mother Theresa

I am sure that each name evoked an emotion within you, based on their reputation. If your name were on this list, would it be a "good name?"

As we study this section of Ecclesiastes, we will observe 7 comparative proverbs or "better than" statements given by Solomon to help lead us to make wise choices.

Let's look at verse 1. What is a good name better than?

When someone is wearing fine perfume and you sit beside them, their aroma is pleasant. In the same way, those with a good name are pleasant and draw others to them.

Now look at the second half of verse 1 through verse 4. How is the house of mourning better than the house of feasting? Is this generally how we think?

Think for a moment, from God's perspective. Those who attend a funeral are sober and thinking about the reality of the brevity of life, while those at a party can become foolish and do things they regret...perhaps even making a "bad name" for themselves.

Paul says in Philippians 1:21, *"For to me to live is Christ, and to die is gain."* And the psalmist wrote in Psalm 116:15, *"Precious in the sight of the Lord is the death of his saints."*

This eternal perspective is not one we naturally have. It only comes from being in God's Word and being reminded over and over, this world is not our home.

Let's observe verses 5 and 6. Why would a wise rebuke be better than the songs or laughter of fools?

Receiving constructive correction is not usually an enjoyable experience but a wise rebuke will accomplish much more in our lives than laughter. Solomon compares the laughter of fools to the crackling of thorns under a pot. They make a lot of noise as they burn but are useless for keeping a fire going.

Have you been rebuked or corrected by someone wiser than you? How did you accept the rebuke? How does our pride and emotions get in the way when we are rebuked?

Let's turn to verses 7-10. According to verse 7, what does oppression and bribery do to a wise man?

The word "mad" in the Hebrew is "halal". It means to rave, to make a show, to boast and thus to be clamorously foolish. Eventually your wise heart will be corrupted because you will be tempted to take a bribe or a short cut to achieve an outcome you desire. Oppression tempts us to leave our wise lifestyle and live like a fool.

Verse 8 contains the last of the comparative proverbs given by Solomon to us in this chapter. What are they?

DISCUSSION QUESTION:

Have you ever begun something that did not end well? What happened and what did you learn from your experience?

We've all heard the phrases, "It is one thing to begin well, but it is another to end well" or "The Christian life is a marathon, not a sprint." In essence, this is what Solomon is teaching in this verse. It is not the one who begins the race with great bravado and pride, but it is the one who humbly and patiently runs the race that God has ordained for him and actually crosses the finish line. He is the winner.

Paul set a great example for all of us. At the end of his life, he said, *"I have fought the good fight, I have finished the race, I have kept the faith."* (2 Timothy 4:7) May we, like Paul, finish our race well.

In closing let's look at verses 9-13. What does verse 9 tell us about anger?

It is important to notice that this verse does not say we should never become angry but rather we are not to be easily provoked into explosive angry outbursts. It is not only foolish but also sinful.

Go to James 1:19-20. What do these verses say about anger? And how can you apply them in your own life today?

In verse 10, we see that the foolish man longs for the "good old days." Life always seems to look better in the rearview mirror. But was it really better than today or do we just selectively remember the past that way? Solomon says this too is foolishness.

In verses 11 and 12, we see an inheritance is a good thing when handled wisely with the help of the Lord. Wisdom is a protection to our lives both physically and spiritually.

And finally, may we remember as verse 13 says, God is in control. We cannot undo what He has done. Like the curse of Genesis 3, God's plans cannot be thwarted.

Is there something you need to release to the Lord today? Give it to Him now in prayer.

Verse of the Day:

Wisdom gives strength to the wise man

more than ten rulers who are in a city.

Ecclesiastes 7:19

Day Five—Choosing What Is Best
Ecclesiastes 7: 14-29

Begin with prayer.

Slowly read or color-code Ecclesiastes 7:14-29.

Knowledge is knowing what is best. Wisdom is choosing to do what is best. **Let's look at verse 14. What are we to consider?**

Prosperity is a gift from the Lord and Solomon says to be joyful. But when adversity comes we are to consider that this too is from the Lord. God uses adversity in our lives to humble us and draw us near to Him. Prosperity is not necessarily always good, and adversity is not necessarily always bad. Both can be blessings in our lives as we learn to surrender to God's will.

Now look at verses 15-18. What does Solomon mean by being overly righteous or overly wicked?

Have you seen an overly righteous person? They are hard to be around. The pride oozes from their mouth and their self-righteousness leads to their own destruction. Ephesians 2:8 & 9 tells us we are saved by grace through faith. Salvation is a gift, not a result of our works, so that no one may boast. May we not become "overly" righteous but fear God and follow His ways.

According to verse 19, what is one wise man stronger than?

According to verse 20, how many have never sinned?

Paul came to this same conclusion in Romans 3:23. He said, *"for all have sinned and fall short of the glory of God."* All mankind is sinful, but God has provided righteousness to us through His Son, Jesus Christ.

As you observe verse 21 and 22, what is Solomon's warning to us?

DISCUSSION QUESTION:

Are you overly sensitive to what others have said about you? Who in your life needs grace because of something they have said negatively about you? Do you ever speak about others behind their backs?

We need to be willing to forgive because at some point, we too will need forgiveness for the unkind words we have spoken about others.

Now look at verses 23-25. Here we see that even though Solomon was given greater wisdom than any other, he still desired even more wisdom. So he continues to seek it out.

That brings us to verse 26 where Solomon observes something more bitter than death. What is he referring to?

Solomon compares the seductress' heart to "snares and nets" and her hands to "fetters" (chains). This woman is a trap! Solomon knows this temptation well since he had 1,000 wives and concubines. According to 1 Kings 11, these women turned Solomon's heart away from the Lord and led him into idolatry.

What happens to the one who pleases the Lord at the end of verse 26?

How have you seen women preying on men and men falling into their trap, in our culture?

May we warn our sons to stay far from her and teach our daughters to never be like her.

In closing, let's look at verses 27 - 29. What had Solomon "sought for repeatedly", but could not find?

A man or woman who pleases the Lord is rare. If Solomon were seeking for one today—would he point at you as one in 1,000?

How did God create man according to verse 29 and what has man done?

Since the fall in the Garden of Eden, man has been chasing after his own pursuits and following his own sinful desires.

Is there an area where you feel ensnared by sin? Let's go to the Lord in prayer and confess and repent of our sin. God, through the Holy Spirit, will give you His strength and wisdom to overcome your desires and areas of temptation.

Week 5~Ecclesiastes 8, 9 & 10:1~10

Verse of the Day:

A man's wisdom

makes his face shine,

Ecclesiastes 8:1

Day 1—It's Time to Shine
Ecclesiastes 8: 1-9

Begin with prayer.

Slowly read or color-code Ecclesiastes 8:1-9.

According to verse 1, how is godly wisdom shown in our appearance?

Verse 1 tells us that wisdom changes the appearance of our face. Our face will shine! In the New Testament, Jesus said in Matthew 5:16, *"In the same way, let your light shine before others, so that they may see your good works and give glory to your Father who is in heaven."*

When we possess God's wisdom, we radiate its light. Just as a child is a reflection of his parents, we reflect our relationship to our Father God by displaying His wisdom in our lives. By doing so, our lives then give glory to God, and we also become a blessing to others.

Does your face shine with godly wisdom in your home, in your workplace, in your church, or in your social circle of friends?

Our time spent with the Lord will not only affect our physical appearance, but our character, our attitude and our daily walk with Christ as we obey His Word, and share it with others. John 13:35 says, *"By this all people will know that you are my disciples, if you have love for one another."* As true believers in Jesus Christ, we must reflect His love to a lost and dying world, and let His light shine through our faces so that everyone we meet will see Christ in us and be drawn to our Lord and Savior.

As we observe verses 2—6, Solomon counsels that a wise man will keep the king's command and submit to his authority. Solomon is speaking of obedience to the king.

According to verse 2, why should a man submit to the king's command?

In this passage, Solomon is most likely referring to an officer or one who serves the king. This man would have taken an oath of allegiance to obey the king in the name of God. Therefore, he is to respect the authority of the king and obey him because he has pledged his loyalty to him.

In I Chronicles 29:24 it says, *"All the leaders and the mighty men, and also all the sons of King David, pledged their allegiance to King Solomon."* In essence, when the people of Israel submitted to and obeyed their king, they were also obeying God.

In verses 3 and 4, Solomon continues to give counsel to the one who serves the king. What did you learn about challenging the king's authority if you disagreed with him?

Because of this truth, even if one did not agree with the king, you still had to approach the king wisely, with appropriate respect and obedience. Therefore, in verse 3, Solomon states that you must not be in a hurry to go from the presence of the king or walk away from him. This would be considered an offense and an act of disobedience for which the king could punish you. Also, in Israel, you would be turning your back and walking away from the king that God had put in authority over you.

As we observe verses 5 and 6, we also learn that timing is everything if we decide to challenge the king's authority (or anyone in authority over us). What does Solomon say a wise person will know and do in these circumstances?

It takes wisdom to know the right thing to do and the right time to do it.

DISCUSSION QUESTION:

Have you ever been under the authority of someone that you did not agree with -- perhaps a spouse, boss, pastor, elder, professor or civil leaders? How did you handle the situation and what was the outcome?

Questioning leadership should be done very carefully, with appropriate respect. A wise person will first pray for God's wisdom and wait patiently as God reveals to us the best course of action to take and the right time to take the action.

In verses 8 and 9, Solomon discusses the limitations that are over earthly rulers. They do not have all power, and their power is not without its limitations. A wise ruler will understand that his power only goes so far.

According to verse 8, what two things do rulers not have power over?

No one can be delivered from or escape the consequences of their own wickedness, not even the king. God is the final judge, and He will hold everyone accountable.

In verse 9, Solomon concludes that these are his observations as he applied his mind to what was done under the sun and as he saw rulers hurting those they ruled over.

How did Peter respond to the government in Acts 5:29?

We may experience injustice in our own lives. May we respond with joy and trust God during these difficult times. Let's close in prayer, asking God to give us wisdom and strength for today.

Verse of the Day:

Each of us

will give an account

of himself to God.

Romans 14:12

Day 2—Our God is Good
Ecclesiastes 8: 10-17

Begin with prayer.

Slowly read or color-code Ecclesiastes 8:10-17.

Have you, like Solomon, been to a funeral of one who did not live a godly lifestyle? As Solomon witnessed the wicked one's burial, what did he observe according to verse 10?

Solomon knew that this wicked person had gone in and out of the "holy place," This person had died, and was being praised in the very city where he had carried out his hypocrisy and wickedness. Solomon concluded, "this also is vanity," a vapor, and meaningless.

The wicked deeds of mankind are not always punished quickly or speedily, either by our earthly justice system or by God. What occurs in "the heart of the children of man," when there is not swift justice?

The "children of man" is a reference to fallen mankind, those who do not know Jesus Christ as their Lord and Savior. Here on earth, "under the sun," when true justice is not quickly carried out, man will continue to sin because he thinks there are no consequences. He believes he has gotten away with his crimes.

God does not always judge mankind immediately. Why would God delay His judgment?

Our God is not only a God of justice, but He is also a God of mercy, grace and patience. He gives time for man to repent of his sins and turn to Him.

John 3:17 says, *"For God did not send his son into the world to condemn the world, but in order that the world might be saved through him."*

However, if a man continues in his evil deeds and does not repent, he faces the certainty of a final day of judgment when he will stand before the Lord and give an account for every evil deed he's committed.

According to Romans 14:12, will the wicked man escape judgment?

Now look back at Ecclesiastes 8. Verses 12 and 13 contrast the "wicked" with "those who fear God." Even though Solomon understood that a sinner could do evil 100 times and still live a long life, what did he know and believe because of his faith in God?

What does it mean to "fear God" and "fear before Him?"

We are to have an awareness or God-consciousness that we are always in the presence of a holy God who is omnipresent, omniscient, and omnipotent. Solomon knew that ultimately "it will be well" with those who live and walk before God in daily obedience because they fear the Lord.

"It will not be well for the wicked" because they do not fear God. They do not live their lives as though they are daily in the presence of the Lord. They have no awareness or consciousness of that truth. It is better to fear the Lord and live a godly life because eventually God will reward the righteous and judge the wicked.

As Solomon points out in verse 14, there is injustice in the world in which we live, and Solomon defined this injustice as "vanity." What did Solomon observe taking place on the earth?

Solomon saw the righteous receive what the wicked deserved, and he saw the wicked receive what the righteous deserved. Basically, the good guy does not always win, and the bad guy does not always lose. Sometimes a cheater does get the better grade, a greedy man does have more money, and deceitful politicians do have more power and popularity. There will be injustice in this world until Jesus Christ returns and sets up His kingdom.

We who are righteous must remember our future reward and blessings that God has promised to us who are faithfully serving, trusting and walking in fear before Him. We must take comfort in His promises to us as we wait *"for our blessed hope, the appearing of the glory of our great God and Savior Jesus Christ."* (Titus 2:13)

DISCUSSION QUESTION:

Whether our lives are just or unjust, as we await the return of Jesus, how does Solomon tell us to live and respond to the days of life that God has given to us under the sun? (See verse 15) How are you living this out in your life?

Once again Solomon tells us to enjoy the everyday, ordinary things of life that God blesses us with. Our God is a good God.

In conclusion, Solomon saw all the work of God under the sun and found it to be incomprehensible. The work of God is beyond human wisdom, and our capacity to know, understand, or explain what God is doing is limited. Our limited ability should humble us because we must accept God's wisdom as superior to ours. It is impossible for any man, even Solomon, the wisest man who ever lived, to understand life under the sun.

May we trust in God's sovereignty today. Let's close with a prayer of thanksgiving to God.

Verse of the Day:

He makes his sun rise

on the evil

and on the good,

and sends rain on the just

and on the unjust.

Matthew 5:45

Day 3—Finding Joy
Ecclesiastes 9: 1-9

Begin with prayer.

Slowly read or color-code Ecclesiastes 9:1-9.

Only God knows what the future holds for each one of us. If you remember from earlier chapters in Ecclesiastes, Solomon has already told us that prosperity is not necessarily always good, and suffering and adversity is not always bad.

As you read verses 2 and 3, does God reward His followers with external earthly blessings while punishing the wicked on earth? What did you learn about the different groups of people recorded in these verses?

Look up Matthew 5:45. What does Jesus say about the just and the unjust?

Have we not seen this to be true by experience in our own lives as we have seen both the godly and the ungodly experience the blessings of God as well as the suffering and sorrow that comes with the troubles of life such as tornadoes, earthquakes, hurricanes, economic disasters, wars, famines, and diseases. It takes godly wisdom and understanding to be able to continue to honor and glorify God both in the good times as well as in the bad times. As we grow and mature in our faith, we are better able to do this.

Let's look at verses 4-6. Solomon says a "living dog is better than a dead lion". What point was Solomon making by comparing these two animals?

At the time Solomon lived, dogs were not household pets as in our culture today, but they were despised animals. Dogs were considered dirty scavengers who roamed the streets. They were wild, not tame. Lions were highly thought of and considered to be noble animals who were honored in Solomon's day. Even so, he said it is better to be a dirty, despised dog who is alive than a powerful, honored lion, but dead. So Solomon's point is that life is better than death.

According to verses 5 and 6, why is living better than dying?

Death is final. Hebrews 9:27 tells us, *"It is appointed for man to die once, and after that comes judgment."* We all have an appointment with death and none of us will escape it.

DISCUSSION QUESTION:

Even though life is difficult and death is certain, how does Solomon encourage us to live our lives while alive on this earth, according to verses 7-9? Are you doing these things? Why or why not?

There was a time in America when having a family meal together, usually at the dinner hour, was considered sacred, a "do not miss" opportunity, but today times have changed and not necessarily for the better.

No longer do families gather together daily around the table to enjoy a relaxing, delicious, healthy meal where they can share the events of the day and show love and support toward one another. Life today is busy! With work and travel schedules, sports practices and games, music lessons, church activities, and technological gadgets, how can we ever find the time to enjoy a meal together without interruptions?

Research shows that eating meals together has great benefits for our families. We must be intentional and try to have as many family members available for a meal as often as possible, throughout the week. We need to set aside our cell phones, computers, and other devices as well as turn off the TV. Instead, light a candle, put on some music, and serve a healthy, delicious meal to your family. Relax, have fun, bond with one another over some great food and drink. It should become your favorite time of the day, and your family will be healthier and happier because of it!

In verse 8, Solomon encourages the people to wear their best clothes and enjoy their celebrations. Putting oil on ones head could have meant bathing or applying perfume and lotions. Enjoy life!

What does Solomon tell husbands to do in verse 9? If you are married, what could you do as a wife to truly enjoy your marriage more?

God is the one who created and designed marriage stating in Genesis 2:18, *"It is not good that the man should be alone; I will make him a helper fit for him."* God created woman and brought her to the man, and in 2:24, we are told, *"a man shall leave his father and his mother and hold fast to his wife, and they shall become one flesh."*

God created marriage for both the man and the woman. We are to find enjoyment and contentment with one another. If you are married, close out today's study in prayer for your husband. Pray for your friendship, faithfulness and bond. Pray that you will find joy together, all the days of your life.

Verse of the Day:

The words of the wise

heard in quiet

are better than the shouting

of a ruler among fools.

Ecclesiastes 9:17

Day 4—The Wisest of All
Ecclesiastes 9: 10-18

Begin with prayer.

Slowly read or color-code Ecclesiastes 9:10-18.

According to verse 10 how is one to do their work?

How does the apostle Paul tell us to do our work in Colossians 3:23?

Whatever work God gives us to do, we are to strive for excellence and do it with all our strength. We aren't to be lazy, but hard, energetic workers, whether we work inside or outside of our homes. When we work in this way, we are actually serving the Lord and it will bring us joy!

Solomon tells us to enjoy our food, drink, family, friends, marriages and work because once we are dead all of this will be no more. We have God's approval to do so! Have fun! Sometimes Christians can be sticks in the mud. No matter where you are, on the mission field or inside your own home, live life enthusiastically and to the fullest! We never know what tomorrow brings. It could be cut short. With the help of the Holy Spirit may we embrace life, serve God with every breath in our lungs and give it all we got!

Observe verses 11 and 12. What are the 5 different human abilities described here and does possessing these, guarantee a successful life under the sun?

Life is unpredictable. Time and chance happen to us all. What does Solomon compare time to in verse 12?

Tell of a time when you made plans but they fell through.

A wise woman once told me when I fell on some hard times, "This may be your plan B for life, but this was God's plan A for you". Sometimes the plans I have are interrupted by the plans God has for me.

Proverbs 19:21 says, *"Many are the plans in the mind of a man, but it is the purpose of the Lord that will stand."*

We must trust God, walk in obedience and faith and enjoy the blessing He gives, both the expected and unexpected!

Let's look at verses 13-16. Solomon tells a short story about a powerful king who attacked a small city. Defeat was certain except there was this poor, wise man who delivered the city by his wisdom yet no one remembered that poor man. He was forgotten!

How did this story impact Solomon?

There are many Biblically wise people who go without recognition or reward every single day. They serve in our churches, schools, communities and on the mission field. They serve the sick and the hungry. They love and listen and take meals to those who need comforted. They counsel, lead children's Sunday school classes, mentor teens and open their homes for fellowship. The world does not call these people wise but they are the wisest of all. They value what God values and though there are few rewards for them here on earth, one day God will reward them.

DISCUSSION QUESTIONS:

Look at Ecclesiastes 9:17. What is the wise way and how is it better? How can you apply this in your life?

Research has shown that when a parent raises their voice at a child—a defense mechanism kicks in that helps the child emotionally protect himself by tuning out the words you are saying. So when we as moms yell, our child has not been brought any closer to wisdom and understanding. Rather than shout, we must speak gently, calmly and quietly. The words of the wise heard in quiet are better than the shouting of a ruler. Plus, we'll feel better about ourselves as a wife and mom.

In closing, look at verse 18. What is wisdom better than?

Wisdom is better than war but one loud mouth sinner can bring much destruction to a city, country or in our case church, business place or home. May we be the one wise voice in the midst of arguments, quarrels and fights. With God's help, may we be the one who can lead people to peace through our gentle words and the wisdom of the Lord.

Verse of the Day:

Righteousness exalts a nation,

but sin is a reproach to any people.

Proverbs 14:34

Day 5—Avoid Folly
Ecclesiastes 10: 1-9

Begin with prayer.

Slowly read or color-code Ecclesiastes 10:1-9.

Read verse 1, like a dead fly in perfume, what does folly do to wisdom?

Have you seen it? A good man or woman ruined by just one poor choice?

Wise people stay away from folly, but some have given in to foolish actions such as entering into an extra-marital affair. As a result, they destroy their own reputations, their marriage and family, and often their careers. Everything they have spent their lifetime building is suddenly gone for a moment of illicit pleasure. Others may decide to drink and drive or text while driving, resulting in a car accident which can cause a lifetime of grief not only for themselves but also for others.

What does verse 2 say the inclination of each heart is?

Spiritually speaking, in the deep secret places of our hearts, only God knows who we really are. Others see us on the outside, and they think they know who we are, but 1 Samuel 16:7 tells us, *"For the Lord sees not as man sees: man looks on the outward appearance, but the Lord looks on the heart."* Our heart is at the very core of our being, and the way our heart leans determines the direction we will go in life.

In what direction is your heart leading you? Does it lead you toward God or away from Him and His ways?

Examine your own heart according to Matthew 22:37.

Verse 3 says the fool is characterized as one who lacks sense. It is obvious to everyone that he's a fool by his behavior. He proves it by walking in the wrong direction, away from God.

As you read through verses 4—7, you will see that he speaks of a ruler who is a fool and exhibits foolish behavior by becoming angry with those serving under him.

DISCUSSION QUESTION:

What practical advice does Solomon give in verse 4 in dealing with the anger of a foolish ruler? How does this apply to us when someone is angry with us?

Remain calm and controlled. As you control your own emotions it should bring a peaceful resolution to the conflict.

What wisdom does Proverbs 15:1 give us for a similar situation?

According to verses 5-7, what are some of the evils under the sun regarding rulers that Solomon has seen?

Leaders are not always wise. Many make errors in judgment. Sometimes incompetent people rise to a position of authority while a wise man sits in a low position.

In light of this, how should we pray for our nation and our leaders?

Proverbs 14:34 says, *"Righteousness exalts a nation, but sin is a reproach to any people."* All of our leaders need our prayers.

In closing, we see in verses 8 -9, a description of daily tasks common to Solomon's culture where the worker was injured because he did not apply wisdom.

What happened to the workers in verses 8 and 9 and why?

These people were all just doing their jobs, but had not taken the proper safety precautions to avoid injury. Also, their skills may have been lacking and they needed more training as well as better equipment or tools.

Let's close out our week of study in prayer for our loved ones and ourselves. Write your prayer below.

Week 6~Ecclesiastes 10:10~20, 11 & 12

Verse of the Day:

The end of the matter;

all has been heard.

Fear God

and keep his commandments,

for this is the whole duty of man.

Ecclesiastes 12:13

Day 1—Working Smarter Not Harder
Eccelsiastes 10: 10-20

Welcome back to week 6! This week we complete our study in Ecclesiastes. I'm so glad you are still studying and going strong!

Let's begin with prayer.

Slowly read or color-code Ecclesiastes 10:10-20.

I remember a conversation I had over lunch with my Greek Professor in college. I shared with him how frustrating it was to attend a Christian college after attending a public school. My passion in high school was to share the gospel, then I went to Bible College and there was no one to share the gospel with! That was terribly frustrating and almost boring for me. I lost my drive, passion and courage, as my Bible became my textbook. My professor answered with his southern accent:

"Courrrrrrrrrtney (he always drew out his "r's"), you must sharpen your ax so when you leave this place, when you hit, you will hit harder."

DISCUSSION QUESTION:

Look at Ecclesiastes 10:10. What happens when an ax is not sharp and how does wisdom help? Do you have something in your life where you need to work smarter not harder?

A wise worker sharpens the edge of a dull ax before trying to use it. Sharpening the ax may take more time but it will save energy in the long run. Do you feel dull, worn down or not very sharp? Perhaps you need a refresher course in an area of your life where you are struggling. Maybe you could purchase a new book on organization, time management or finances; perhaps you could find a mentor in the area of the trade you work in or take an on-line class. Wisdom helps one succeed!

Look at verse 11. What does it teach us about timing?

The snake charmer had to act quickly, without delay, otherwise he would be bitten and lose his wages and perhaps his life! We must apply wisdom at just the right time for it to be successful. Foolishly delaying can bring needless suffering to our lives.

In verses 12-15, we see the gracious words of the wise contrasted with the senseless words of a fool. What do the wise man's words do for the wise man?

List some of the qualities of the fool's words below.

A wise woman should be giving words of praise and glory to God because of her personal relationship with Jesus Christ, as she draws others to Christ by her testimony. When speaking to people, her words are gracious, humble, encouraging, building others up and not tearing them down, speaking the truth in love with kindness, gentleness and patience. She is self disciplined and controls her temper and her tongue.

A fool's words consume him. His words are not only destructive to others, but are also self-destructive, leading to his own downfall. His words are senseless, silly and foolish and then progress to evil madness. By the time he's finished talking, everyone knows he's a fool.

Solomon says this fool is extremely ignorant, so much so, that "he does not know the way to the city." (v. 15) This fool who is so prideful and boastful about life cannot even find his own way into town. That may be the same reason that his toil wearies him. He probably works harder, but not necessarily smarter!

Which are you? Do you speak with wise words or do you sometimes go the foolish man's route?

Oh friends, I'm a woman of many words as I mentioned in the introduction. I have come a long way but only by the renewing of my mind daily with God's Word. He has changed me but it is still a daily struggle for me to choose wisdom over folly in my word choices.

Let's skip ahead for a moment to verse 20 since it deals with words as well. How does verse 20 warn us?

Beware. Words you think you are saying in secret could become public knowledge, bringing dire consequences. Always measure your words and be wise even when you think what you are saying will be kept private.

In closing, let's look at verses 16-19. Solomon contrasts the strong, effective leader with the weak, ineffective leader. What are their qualities?

Consider, how does this apply not only in a kingdom but in a home, church, or workplace?

Solomon himself was very young when he began ruling as Israel's king, but he understood his need for wisdom. He prayed, asking God to grant it to him, which God did. This in turn, brought blessing upon the nation of Israel during Solomon's reign.

DISCUSSION QUESTION:

Let's consider our own lifestyles for a moment. How do we begin the day? Do we indulge in feasting or drunkenness? Do we put off tasks? Are we eating to be stronger or to pass time? How is your home? Verse 18 says the roof is sagging and leaking. Are we keeping it up?

Solomon says in verse 19, "money answers everything." If one is lazy and spends her days partying rather than working, she's not likely to have much money to purchase bread. Eventually, the money runs out. So Solomon points out the wisdom of work and contrasts it with the foolishness of laziness.

Do you have a long to-do list to complete? Let's say a prayer over it now. May we work hard today, to the glory of God in all we do!

Verse of the Day:

Whoever sows sparingly

will also reap sparingly,

and whoever sows bountifully

will also reap bountifully.

2 Corinthians 9:6

Day 2—Living By Faith
Ecclesiastes 11: 1-5

Let's begin with prayer.

Slowly read or color-code Ecclesiastes 11:1-5.

Let's look at verses 1 and 2. Commentaries explain that this refers to doing business in grain by putting it on a ship and having it set sail to be traded—casting it on the waters. The merchant harvested his crop, sent it off to sell, and then received back a dividend.

Do you see any risks in following Solomon's advice in verse one?

When the merchant sends out his ship, he cannot control what will happen on the water. The weather is unpredictable, and storms could come up, causing a shipwreck. There could be enemy ships that attack and steal the cargo. But the ships could also safely arrive at their destinations, and return back bringing rich imports and needed goods.

What else will a wise merchant/trader do according to verse 2?

Because disasters are possible, he will diversify, sending out his cargo among seven or eight different ships. He is then much more likely to receive a return on his investment, rather than losing it all, if he sends all his cargo out on only one ship.

Let's consider these verses spiritually. Life offers no guarantees to any of us as Solomon states in verse 2, "for you know not what disaster may happen on earth." However, that does not give us an excuse for inactivity. Even though we cannot control future circumstances, we are not to withdraw from living life by crawling into our beds and pulling the covers over our heads!

Verses one and two each begin with an action word. We are to "cast," and we are to "give." God wants us to live our lives without fear of the future and with passion and enthusiasm. We are to step out of our comfort zones and serve others, as well as the Lord. Sometimes this may involve taking risks, but we do it through faith in Him and all for His glory.

Re-read verses 3 through 6.

Just as the merchant of verses 1 and 2 had to take risks in order to be successful, so does the farmer. Much of a farmer's bountiful harvest is dependent upon the weather, which as we said earlier, is unpredictable and uncontrollable by man. Therefore, the farmer is completely at the mercy of nature, at the mercy of a cloud filled with rain or of trees falling over.

If a farmer becomes cautious and overly concerned about the weather, what does verse 4 say he will not do?

Verse 4 speaks of the farmer who constantly worries about the weather, waiting for just the right time or perfect circumstances to plant or harvest. If it is too windy, he'll not go out to sow or plant his seeds. If it looks like rain, he'll not go out to reap his harvest. If he waits too long, he'll miss his opportunity to sow his seed, and then, of course, he'll have nothing to harvest.

This is a principle recorded all throughout Scripture.

Read 2 Corinthians 9:6. What does it say about sowing seeds?

DISCUSSION QUESTION:

What kind of excuses do we often make for not serving the Lord, for not sowing and trusting God for the harvest?

We often say we are too young, too old, too busy, uneducated or ill equipped. We will say the timing isn't right, and we will end up waiting a whole lifetime, until it is too late. We will end up accomplishing nothing for the Lord. God wants us to get busy for Him. God asks only for our faithfulness because any success or harvest that comes is up to Him. As the Apostle Paul reminded the Corinthian church in 1 Corinthians 3:6, "I planted, Apollos watered, but God gave the growth." Therefore, all glory goes to God and God alone.

Verse 5 speaks of God as the Creator of everything. No one can completely understand how a child is formed in the womb of its mother. It is a miracle. We have modern technology and ultrasounds available to us today to observe a child growing in his mother's womb. **Even so, what does Solomon specifically say we do not know about a pre-born child in verse 5?**

It is beyond our ability to comprehend how the spirit (this word could also be translated breath) comes into our bodies. This is a mystery that only our Creator God can explain.

Ecclesiastes 12:7 speaks of our spirit returning to God, who gave it, upon our death. The ESV says, *"and the dust returns to the earth as it was, and the spirit returns to God who gave it."*

Here's two more places where we see this truth in scripture.

Acts 7:59 says, *"And as they were stoning Stephen, he called out, "Lord Jesus, receive my spirit."*

Luke 23:46 says, *"Then Jesus, calling out with a loud voice, said, "Father, into your hands I commit my spirit."*

God breathes into every living being the breath of life. When we draw our final breath on earth, our spirit will return to God, the Giver of life. On that day, when we see God face to face, may we be found faithful. Let's close in prayer, asking God to give us more faith for the journey ahead.

Verse of the Day:

Do not be anxious about anything,

but in everything by prayer and supplication

with thanksgiving

let your requests be made known to God.

Philippians 4:6

Day 3—It's Good to Be Alive
Ecclesiastes 11: 6-10

Let's begin with prayer.

Slowly read or color-code Ecclesiastes 11:6-10.

What instructions does Solomon give in verse 6?

Be a faithful, hard worker everyday, all day. As we have seen, God is in control as to whether we prosper or not. Our responsibility is to faithfully serve Him, morning, noon and night. Then we patiently wait, like the farmer, to reap a harvest.

As we continue observing verses 7-10, we see that Solomon is a realist. He does not look at life through "rose colored" glasses or try to sugarcoat his view of life in any way. He paints a picture showing both the positive and negative aspects of every season of life.

In verse 7, what is sweet and pleasant?

When we wake in the morning, rejoice and be glad! It's good to be alive!

What advice does Solomon give in verse 8?

If God chooses to give us a long life, then we are to rejoice in all the years of our life, even old age. Why? Because the longer we live, the more opportunity we have to serve the Lord. Also, we have more time to spend with our family and friends and to do the work God has given us to do.

Because Solomon is a realist, what does he also say we must "remember" in verse 8?

There are "days of darkness" leading into old age. The aging process begins to take a toll on the human body, and eventually, this will lead to death.

Solomon, having spoken to those who are older, now speaks to the young and advises them in the same way. They too are to rejoice in the days of their youth.

In the latter half of verse 9, what words of wisdom, followed by a warning, does Solomon give to the young?

Solomon is saying to enjoy the pleasures of life that come with being young. All of your future is ahead of you, so follow your heart, dream dreams, and try to fulfill them. Don't wait until you are older to start enjoying your life.

But do not let your heart lead you into sin, and do not satisfy the desires or the lusts of your flesh (Galatians 5:16-17). Instead, walk in holiness and obedience to God's Word because there is a day coming when all will give an account before God, for how they have lived their lives.

According to verse 10, what must be removed from a young person's life so they can experience true joy?

A vexation is anything that causes you inner turmoil and anguish. If you are mentally upset, worried, angry, depressed, bitter, resentful, or anxious, then you are vexed.

One cure for this is to go to the Word of God and to pray. Philippians 4:6-7 are wonderful verses with a command and a promise. The command is, "do not be anxious about anything, but in everything by prayer and supplication with thanksgiving, let your requests be known to God." The promise is, "And the peace of God, which surpasses all understanding, will guard your hearts and minds in Christ Jesus."

We are also to put away anything, especially sinful things, that weaken our body and make us ill. Things such as gluttony, drinking alcohol to excess, drugs, sexual immorality, lack of rest and exercise. God wants us to have strong, healthy bodies with which to serve Him. We are to take good care of ourselves, wisely choosing a healthy lifestyle, putting away anything that harms our body and brings it pain. Remember the Apostle Paul told us in 1 Corinthians 6:19-20 that our body is a temple of the Holy Spirit, so we are to glorify God in our body.

Solomon closes out chapter 11 by stating in verse 10, "for youth and the dawn of life are vanity." What point is Solomon making here?

Solomon is not saying that our younger years are meaningless. He's saying that our youthful years go by very quickly, like a vapor. We are only considered young for a short while. Before we know it, we are middle aged, and then soon after, we become senior citizens moving into our elderly years, if God is gracious and gives us length of days.

DISCUSSION QUESTION:

We have seen in Ecclesiastes 11 that Solomon has encouraged us to enjoy every season of life right where we are. What has been your favorite season and why?

Don't wait for tomorrow to come. Rejoice in the Lord, and make the most of today. That is "wisdom for living well!"

Verse of the Day:

Vanity of vanities,

says the Preacher;

all is vanity.

Ecclesiastes 12:8

Day 4—Remember God In Your Youth
Ecclesiastes 12: 1-8

Let's begin with prayer.

Slowly read or color-code Ecclesiastes 12:1-8.

We have come to the final chapter in our study of the book of Ecclesiastes. Solomon, the son of King David, reigned over God's chosen people, the nation of Israel, for 40 years as their king. As we have seen, Solomon asked himself many of the same questions that we have asked ourselves as we have searched for the meaning of our lives.

All of us at some point in time have asked: Who am I? Why am I here? What is the purpose of my life on this earth?

At the end of chapter 12, Solomon will give his final, closing thoughts to these questions, and we need to heed his advice.

Let's look at verse 1. Who are we to remember in our youth?

While we still have our whole life ahead of us, it is wise to choose to follow God, to love, serve, honor and obey Him while living for His glory, all the days of our life. Beginning when we are young, we are to lay a strong spiritual foundation because days and years are coming in which we will say, "I have no pleasure in them."

Following our youthful years, the aging process begins. Solomon describes these years by making some interesting comparisons or metaphors, ultimately ending in the physical death of our bodies.

What happens to our bodies as we age according to verses 3 through 7?

In verse 3, our hands and arms tremble, our legs weaken, and we walk stooped or bent over. "Grinders" is a reference to lost teeth, and dimmed "windows" means we have diminished eyesight. We cannot see as well as we did when we were young.

In verse 4, the "doors" shut could mean our mouth is closed because we do not have much to say. The "sound of grinding is low" could mean it is hard to chew (without some of our teeth), so we do not eat as much. We rise in the morning at the sound of the birds because we do not sleep as soundly as we once did. "The daughters of song are brought low," could mean we either no longer have a strong voice with which to sing or our ears can no longer hear music.

In verse 5, the elderly fear "what is high" because they fear falling down and also worry about "terrors," dangerous occurrences that could happen along the way. "The almond tree blossoms" with white blossoms, is a reference to our graying hair. The "grasshopper drags itself along," as we slow down with less energy and enthusiasm for life. "Desire fails" could be referencing a loss of sexual desire or a lack of appetite for food.

According to verse 5, why are all of these things happening to us?

We are nearing the end of our earthly lives. "The mourners go about the streets" sorrowing over our death.

Verse 6 shows the fine line between life and death and how fragile our human bodies really are. We can be gone in an instant through a massive heart attack, stroke, a tragic accident, or various other reasons.

DISCUSSION QUESTION:

Do you struggle with the aging process and in what ways and why?

You are not alone. Research shows that over 11 billion dollars were spent in 2012 on plastic surgery. Our society is obsessed with youth. Everyone tries to look young and no one wants to be considered old! Large sums of money are spent on cosmetics, hair dye, and gym memberships to look young. There is nothing wrong with taking care of our bodies and our physical appearance but we have to be careful that it does not become an idol or source of pride in our lives. We need to age gracefully and appropriately remembering that no matter how much we battle the aging process, eventually it will overtake us and we will have to give in to it.

According to verse 7, what happens to our physical body and spirit when we die?

Solomon closes his comments about our lives coming to an end by stating in verse 8, "Vanity of vanities, says the Preacher; all is vanity."

A life lived under the sun without God is meaningless, a vapor, here today and gone tomorrow, only to be forgotten. But for those who have placed their faith in Jesus Christ, our lives do have meaning and purpose. When we die and leave this earth, we go to our heavenly home to be with our Lord and Savior, Jesus Christ, for all eternity.

Give praise to your Creator now and remember Him all the days of your life! Let's be wise women, who are living well.

Verse of the Day:

For God will bring

every deed into judgment,

with every secret thing,

whether good or evil.

Ecclesiastes 12:14.

Day 5—Fear God and Keep His Commandments
Ecclesiastes 12: 9-14

We have arrived to the final day of study! Way to go!

Let's begin with prayer.

Slowly read or color-code Ecclesiastes 12:9-14.

As we observe verses 9 and 10, we see that either Solomon is talking about himself, or someone else is describing the Preacher. What do these verses tell us about Solomon?

In verse 11, what are the words of the wise compared to?

A goad is a sharp, pointy instrument that was used to push or move an animal along. Solomon used wise words to motivate people to seek the truth about God through His Word. Wise words are also compared to "nails firmly fixed". Nails are used to hold something in place securely.

According to the end of verse 11, who gave Solomon these words?

This is a reference to God. God Himself is our teacher through His Word. God's Word is truth, and we can securely rest in it.

What is the warning to Solomon's son and to us in verse 12?

Today, there are so many books written about God. We can weary ourselves trying to read and study all of them. But there is only ONE book we need to read, study, memorize, meditate on and pray back to God, and that is the very Word of God, the Holy Bible. God's Word alone holds the truth of God's Son, Jesus Christ, and will lead us to salvation in Him.

Look up 2 Timothy 3:16-17. What does it say about God's Word?

We've arrived at Solomon's final closing comments and words of advice to us. At the end of the day, after all has been said and done, what does Solomon conclude in verses 13 and 14?

Fear God.

Keep His commandments.

Why? God will hold us accountable for how we choose to live our lives, whether it be for God or for ourselves, whether our deeds be done in secret or in public, whether they be good or evil.

If we want a life that brings us satisfaction, contentment, meaning and fulfillment, we will wisely choose to live lives of obedience, walking in the fear of the Lord, giving Him all the glory as "women living well."

DISCUSSION QUESTIONS:

What have you learned about life from reading Ecclesiastes?

What have you learned about God from reading Ecclesiastes?

What changes have you made or will you make in your life based on the truths you have learned in your study of the book of Ecclesiastes? Do any of your priorities need to change in order to be a woman of wisdom who is living well?

Thank you for your faithfulness to complete this study.

I pray that you live wisely and live well, all the days of your life!

Keep walking with the King!

Special Thanks

We want to thank the women from the Bible study group at Maranatha Bible Church in Akron, Ohio, for piloting this Ecclesiastes study. Your careful study and feedback was a huge blessing as we created this study.

~ Courtney and Beverly

Video One — Notes

Video Two—Notes

Video Three—Notes

Video Four—Notes

Video Five—Notes

Video Six—Notes

Made in the USA
Middletown, DE
13 February 2018